Common Core Literacy Lesson Plans

Ready-to-Use Resources, 6–8

Eye On Education
6 Depot Way West, Suite 106
Larchmont, NY 10538
(914) 833-0551
(914) 833-0761 Fax
www.eyeoneducation.com

For information about permission to reproduce selections from this book, write
Eye On Education, Permissions Department, Suite 106, 6 Depot Way West,
Larchmont, New York 10538

Library of Congress Cataloging-in-Publication Data

Common core literacy lesson plans : ready-to-use resources, 6-8.
       p.   cm.
Includes bibliographical references.
ISBN 978-1-59667-224-6
1. Language arts (Elementary)—Curricula—United States.
2. Language arts (Middle School)—Curricula—United States.
3. Language arts (Elementary)—Standards—United States.
4. Language arts (Middle School)—Standards—United States.
I. Eye on Education (Firm)
LB1576.C5787 2012
372.6—dc23   2012025665

Contributing Writer: Lesli J. Favor, PhD
Sponsoring Editor: Robert Sickles
Production Editor: Lauren Davis
Copy Editor: Kathleen White
Designer and Compositor: Matthew Williams, click! Publishing Services
Cover Designer: Dave Strauss, 3FoldDesign

10 9 8 7 6 5 4 3 2 1

Also Available from Eye On Education

Common Core Literacy Lesson Plans:
Ready-to-Use Resources, K–5
Ed. Lauren Davis

Common Core Literacy Lesson Plans:
Ready-to-Use Resources, 9–12
Ed. Lauren Davis

Teaching Critical Thinking:
Using Seminars for 21st Century Literacy
Terry Roberts and Laura Billings

Rigor Made Easy:
Getting Started
Barbara R. Blackburn

Rigor Is Not a Four-Letter Word
Barbara R. Blackburn

Math in Plain English:
Literacy Strategies for the Mathematics Classroom
Amy Benjamin

But I'm Not a Reading Teacher:
Strategies for Literacy Instruction in the Content Areas
Amy Benjamin

Vocabulary at the Core:
Teaching the Common Core Standards
Amy Benjamin and John T. Crow

Teaching Grammar:
What Really Works
Amy Benjamin and Joan Berger

Awakening Brilliance in the Writer's Workshop:
Using Notebooks, Mentor Texts, and the Writing Process
Lisa Morris

Active Literacy Across the Curriculum
Heidi Hayes Jacobs

About the Editor

Lauren Davis, Senior Editor at Eye On Education, develops and edits books for teachers and school leaders on literacy and the Common Core State Standards. Lauren is a regular contributor to Eye On Education's blog and is the author of a bimonthly column called "Comments on the Common Core State Standards." She also presents on that topic. Recently, she was one of three judges for Education World's Community Lesson Plan Contest.

Prior to working for Eye On Education, Lauren served as Senior Editor of Weekly Reader's *Current Events*, a classroom news magazine for students in grades 6–12. She also spent five years as Director of Language Arts at Amsco School Publications, a publisher of workbooks and other resources for secondary students.

Lauren has a master's degree in English Education from New York University. She began her career in the classroom, teaching 7th and 11th grade English in New York City. She also taught 6th grade English language arts in Westchester, New York. She is passionate about engaging students in learning.

Special Thanks

The editor would like to thank Lesli Favor for her significant contributions to this book. Lesli is a former English professor who now writes full-time for publishers of books for school classrooms and libraries. She is the author of 59 English/language arts texts, nonfiction books, and leveled readers.

Contents

Part 2: Writing

Part 3: Speaking and Listening

Part 4: Language

Handouts

Free Downloads

The handouts in this book are also available on Eye On Education's website as Adobe Acrobat files. Permission has been granted to purchasers of this book to download and print these handouts for free.

You can access the downloads by visiting Eye On Education's website: www.eyeoneducation.com. From the homepage, locate this book's product page by searching for the book title. Then click the link called "Log in to Access Supplemental Downloads" near the top of the page.

Your book-buyer access code is **CCL-7224-6**.

Index of Free Downloads

Note to Teachers

As your school switches over to the Common Core State Standards, you are likely wondering how your classroom will look different and how your lessons will change. Eye On Education is here to help. *Common Core Literacy Lesson Plans* provides a variety of engaging and easy-to-implement lesson plans based on the standards. You can teach these lessons as they appear, or you can modify them to fit your particular needs. The book also provides ideas for revamping your current lessons to make sure they meet the standards and for creating new lessons to meet additional standards.

These lesson plans emphasize rigorous texts, questions, and tasks, which are at the heart of the Common Core. They also stress authenticity and metacognition. Students need authentic assignments that reflect the kind of work they'll be asked to do beyond school doors. They also need to understand how they are learning so they can eventually do it on their own. Authenticity and metacognition increase engagement. When students become aware of their learning processes and see the value in what they're being assigned, they take more ownership in what they are doing and are more motivated to work hard.

How to Use This Book

This book is intended for grades 6 through 8 teachers, literacy coaches, and curriculum leaders. The lessons can be used in English and across the content areas. Interdisciplinary connections are included for many of the lessons because the standards emphasize the importance of literacy across the curriculum.

The lesson plans include reproducible handouts and links for further resources, and they can be extended from single lessons into full units (we provide ideas on how to do this). You can use each lesson as is, and you will learn how to create your own lessons based on these ideas. In that way, you will get a lot out of this book even when you are done teaching the lesson plans.

The book is organized by the strands of the Common Core State Standards—reading, writing, speaking and listening, and language. However, that sorting system indicates only the *main* emphasis for each lesson. In reality, each lesson incorporates more than one area. Reading, writing, speaking and listening, and language are integrated skills in the real world; they should be taught that way too.

Lesson plans are in order according to grade and skill level. Each lesson plan includes the following information:

- **Grade Level**—the main grade or grades for which the lesson is appropriate

- **Time Frame**—approximate number of class periods to complete the lesson. If you use extension ideas, time frames may be longer.

- **Overview**—general information about the goal and focus of the lesson and how to adapt it to other grades if applicable

- **Common Core State Standards**—Most of the lessons cover more than one standard because the standards are not meant to be taught in isolation. Note that we listed the standards the main lesson covers, but if you choose to extend the lesson based on the suggestions provided, you will incorporate even more standards.

- **Objectives**—what students will learn

- **Background Knowledge Required**—what students need to know before delving into the lesson

- **Materials Needed**—texts and other materials to have on hand for the lesson

- **Agenda**—detailed, step-by-step instructions for the lesson

- **Differentiation**—ideas to adapt the lesson for struggling and advanced learners

- **Assessment**—assessment ideas, including rubrics and scoring guides

- **Notes**—a place for you to reflect on what worked with the lesson and what you would change the next time

Reading

Overview

To teach the Common Core State Standards in reading, you don't have to toss all your wonderful literature lessons and start from scratch. But you do need to look at your lessons and see if they match the rigor level the standards now require. If they don't, see what you can do to make them more challenging. Begin by making sure that your texts are complex enough and that they span the different genres the CCSS require. If they don't, see what you can swap out. Then look at how you teach the readings. The Common Core requires that students spend a great deal of time on the language of the text and that they respond to higher-level, text-based questions and tasks. If you teach *Romeo and Juliet* by having students make personal connections to the theme of love, that's fine, but move that toward the end of your unit. Don't spend too much time at the beginning on the very general questions. Start with a closer look at Shakespeare's language, and make sure that students refer to the text when they answer questions and make inferences. For more tips to keep in mind when revising your lessons or creating new lessons, read the checklist below.

Planning Checklist

When planning a CCSS-based reading lesson, remember these tips:

☐ Choose more complex texts. According to page 4 of the Common Core State Standards Appendix A, you should consider these three areas when choosing complex texts:

- Qualitative measures—your professional judgment about a text's quality. Does the text have levels of meaning, such as satire? What's the purpose of the text, and what background knowledge is required?
- Quantitative measures—a more technical way to rate a text. You can use a scale such as a Lexile, which looks at word frequency and sentence length.
- Reader to text/task—your judgment as a teacher who knows your students! For example, is the text developmentally appropriate for your students?

Make sure to consider all three areas; don't rely on Lexiles alone. Lexiles can be misleading. For example, Hemingway's *The Sun Also Rises* has a grade 2 Lexile level because the language is relatively simple. However, you would never teach it in that grade. Use your professional judgment when choosing complex texts.

☐ Measure students' reading levels and monitor their progress throughout the year. You can use running records such as the Developmental Reading Assessment, Qualitative Reading Inventory, or Fountas and Pinnell Benchmark Assessment System. Or you can do your own fluency check by having students read something at the high end of the Common Core recommendations and then check for accuracy, fluency, and comprehension. Make a plan in your mind for how you'd like students to progress, and monitor them throughout the year (Calkins, Ehrenworth, & Lehman, 2012, p. 43).

☐ Teach short, challenging texts that can be read and reread so that students have plenty of opportunities to ponder meaning. Also teach extended readings so that students learn "stamina and persistence" while reading (Coleman and Pimentel, p. 4).

☐ If you haven't been doing so already, make sure to include literary nonfiction in your curriculum. Literary nonfiction, according to the Common Core, means stories built on arguments and with informational text structures, not stories and memoirs.

☐ Teach texts from a variety of "genres, cultures, and centuries" (Common Core State Standards, p. 35).

☐ Assign text-dependent tasks and questions. Help students learn to make valid inferences with text support.

☐ Provide opportunities for students to compare and synthesize multiple sources.

☐ Analyze informational and argumentative aspects of a story, not just its literary features (such as plot, setting, character, etc.).

☐ Create questions that build in a logical sequence. Don't start too broadly (as can happen with some kinds of prereading questions); pose questions that focus on the details of a text. After that, you can go broader and ask for students' opinions and personal connections.

☐ Some students will need scaffolding to understand complex texts. Scaffolding should not consist of "translating" a story or providing a brief synopsis for students to read ahead of time. Instead, scaffolding should help students with words and phrases so that they can determine meaning on their own. Here are some additional strategies for helping struggling readers.

Strategies to Help Struggling Readers

- Model thinking aloud. For example, say, "I'm not sure I understand this word. But the author is writing about tornadoes, and the sentence right after uses the word *strength*, so I'm paying attention to how powerful tornadoes are."

- Focus on syntax. Students might need practice linking the subject to the verb. In complex texts, such as Shakespeare, the predicate often precedes the subject, which can be confusing for students. They might need to mark the subject and verb until they learn how to read that kind of language more readily.

- Have students annotate the text as they read.

- Have students read some short texts (or small chunks of a text at a time) and reread them several times to ponder meaning. They can also listen to an audio version or read a text aloud to gain additional meaning.

- Teach when (and how) to use context clues and when to use reference sources to check word meanings.

- Use text sets. Following is an example from Barbara Blackburn's *Rigor Made Easy* (2012).

  > After reading the fictional book *The Watsons Go to Birmingham—1963*, by Christopher Paul Curtis, students can read nonfiction online, encyclopedia articles, and/or magazine articles to compare the story to Birmingham, Alabama, during the civil rights period. You could add another step by reading current newspaper and magazine articles to compare it to Birmingham today, detailing the changes that have occurred. (p. 24)

- Allow time for recreational reading, not just methodical close readings. Students need to learn to read for different purposes, including for entertainment.

- Create prereading activities as long as they do not spoil or give away the meaning and ideas of the text. Prereading activities might include help with vocabulary or with background information.

Lesson Plans at a Glance

The Text Is a Gold Mine— Let's Start Digging!

Answering Text-Based Questions

Grade Levels: 6–8

Time Frame: Approximately two class periods

Overview: The Common Core requires that students identify evidence in a text to answer questions about that text. This is a shift from past pedagogical practices of asking for opinions, general observations, and personal responses that can be expressed without combing through a text's words, sentences, and paragraphs. Text-based questions enable deep discussions that require students to grapple with the words and ideas on the page in order to create meaning from the text. This lesson focuses on asking and answering text-based questions. It uses "The Apotheosis of Martin Luther King" as the focus text, but you can use some or all of any complex text (literary or informational) that students are reading. You may want to consult with a social studies teacher and use a text that students are reading in that class.

Common Core State Standards

- 6: Reading, Informational Text, Standard 1: Cite textual evidence to support analysis of what the text says explicitly as well as inferences drawn from the text.

- 7: Reading, Informational Text, Standard 1: Cite several pieces of textual evidence to support analysis of what the text says explicitly as well as inferences drawn from the text.

- 8: Reading, Informational Text, Standard 1: Cite the textual evidence that most strongly supports an analysis of what the text says explicitly as well as inferences drawn from the text.

Objectives

- Students will read a complex text and answer questions that require close analysis of what the words, sentences, and paragraphs in the text are saying.

Background Knowledge Required

No particular background knowledge is required for this lesson.

Materials Needed

- Copies of the first three paragraphs of "The Apotheosis of Martin Luther King," by Elizabeth Hardwick, preferably copies that students can mark up. You can find the essay in *The Best American Essays of the Century*, edited by Joyce Carol Oates and Robert Atwan.

- Copies of the handout: Answering a Text-Based Question Step-by-Step, p. 10

Agenda

1. **Introduction**: Tell students that today they will spend time reading and discussing a short excerpt from an essay. Write the title of the essay on the board. Underline the words *Martin Luther King*. Ask students to briefly explain who this person was. Next, underline the word *apotheosis*. Tell students that this word means "the raising of a person to the level of a god." Finally, pass out copies of the first three paragraphs of the essay (make sure the copies include the title and author of the piece).

2. **Independent Reading**: Ask students to read the passage independently. Encourage them to use active reading strategies that they may know, such as placing check-marks or question marks in the margin and underlining unfamiliar words.

3. **Full-Class Reading**: Ask students to listen and follow along on their copies as you read the passage aloud. Speak clearly and carefully, allowing students to hear the pronunciation of unfamiliar words and to hear the rhythm and cadence of the piece.

4. **Full-Class Discussion**: Lead students through an analysis of the text by asking a series of text-based questions. Each question should cause students to return to the text to reread a word, sentence, or paragraph in order to gather the facts or reasons needed to construct an answer. Text-based questions may ask why an author uses a certain turn of phrase, why the author begins with or emphasizes a certain point, how an author illustrates or defends a point, how word choices create a particular tone or mood, which details reveal or support a theme, and so on. Here are some suggested questions:

   - Why does the author start with this description of Memphis if she plans to raise King to the level of a god?
   - The first sentence states that Memphis "lay . . . under a siege." Based on details in these three paragraphs, do you think the siege is literal or symbolic? Which details help you answer the question?
   - In the first paragraph, the author compares Memphis to a film set. Why does she make this comparison?
   - What does the author mean by "humidity of smugness" in the third paragraph?

5. **Wrap-Up**: Have students complete the handout, following guidelines of your choosing (e.g., independently or in small groups, in class or as homework).

Extend the Lesson

- Don't worry if you don't have time to cover all the questions during class time. You can use the additional questions to extend the lesson to another day, in a homework assignment, or as essay-test questions.

- Repeat the reading and discussion process with the next two paragraphs in the essay, using text-based questions that you create.

- Ask students to write text-based questions of their own, either in small groups or independently. The text could be the first three paragraphs of the essay, or you could assign the next two paragraphs and ask that the questions be based on that section. Use students' questions to demonstrate that a close reading of a text hinges on individual words, phrases, sentences, and ideas. If students stray from text-based questions, explain that forming a personal opinion or judgment or describing one's personal reaction to the text is not the same thing as digging into exactly what the author is saying. Tell students that normally, a person can't ad-lib a response to a text-based question. Wrap up by having students answer one of the student-generated questions, either in writing or in an oral response.

Differentiation

For students who need extra support

- Spend more time helping students work out the meanings of unfamiliar words. Use various strategies such as context clues, peer input, and reference sources. Use class time to allow small groups to tackle one paragraph from the excerpt, discussing and verifying the meaning of each keyword. Then have the groups report back to the full class.

- As homework, students could write paragraphs answering one of the text-based questions that you discussed in class. This reinforces the message that close textual readings require multiple readings of the same passage. A reader's understanding of the text deepens over time.

For advanced students

- Ask for volunteers to read the passage aloud during the full-class reading. You could break the reading assignments into title, author, and heading of place and date, which allows a student to pronounce *apotheosis* properly for the class; paragraph one; paragraph two; paragraph three.

- As homework, students might write paragraphs answering a text-based question that you did not discuss in class. As with struggling students, the advanced students will receive the message that multiple readings are beneficial, but they also will be challenged to find new connections and meaning in the text.

Assessment

- Check students' work on the handout to make sure they responded fully to all five steps of the process. Provide additional tips and examples for steps that students struggle with.

- Use the following rubric to evaluate students' written or oral responses to a text-based question.

Score 4.0	The student ■ Uses multiple words, phrases, or sentences in the text to answer the question. ■ Logically links the evidence (above) to the text-based question. ■ Expresses a clear answer to the question using the evidence and logic in the previous bullets. No major errors or omissions in the score 4.0 content.
Score 3.5	The student demonstrates success at the 3.0 level plus partial success at the 4.0 level.
Score 3.0	The student ■ Uses at least one word, phrase, or sentence in the text in the response. ■ Logically links the evidence (above) to the text-based question. ■ Attempts to express an answer to the question. No major errors or omissions in the score 3.0 content.
Score 2.5	The student demonstrates success at the 2.0 level plus partial success at the 3.0 level.
Score 2.0	The student ■ Refers vaguely to ideas in the text to answer the question. ■ Links (however loosely) the evidence (above) to the text-based question. No major errors or omissions in the score 2.0 content.
Score 1.5	The student demonstrates partial success at the 2.0 level; responses may identify evidence in the text but the student may fail to use it to answer the question or may answer the question without using specific evidence from the text.
Score 1.0	With help, the student achieves partial success at score 2.0 and 3.0 contents; responses are simplistic and limited.
Score 0.5	With help, the student achieves partial success at score 2.0 content but not score 3.0 content.
Score 0.0	Even with help, the student has no success.

Additional Resources

■ You can find a list of curriculum exemplars for asking and answering text-based questions at the Engage New York website. Click through to an exemplar at your grade level to see a lesson plan, including the text and suggested text-based questions: engageny.org/resource/curriculum-exemplars.

■ This page has an 11-minute video in which David Coleman, a contributing author to the Common Core, participates in a discussion about the role of text-based questions in classroom practice: engageny.org/resource/common-core-in-ela-literacy-shift-4-text-based-answers.

Notes

After implementing the lesson, reflect on what worked and what you would change next time.

_____

_____

_____

_____

Answering a Text-Based Question Step-by-Step

1. Write the question that you are asked to answer.

2. Underline keywords in the question that will help you focus your response. For example, does the question ask *why*, ask you to *compare* two things, or give a quotation from the text?

3. Reread the text. As you do so, list words, phrases, sentences, and/or ideas in the text that can help you answer the question.

    ▪

    ▪

    ▪

    ▪

    ▪

4. Think about how the evidence you gathered in step 3 can help you answer the question. Which pieces of evidence are strongest? Which link most logically to the question? Place checkmarks by the strongest pieces of evidence.

5. Write your response to the question using the strongest pieces of evidence. Be sure to link each piece of evidence to the question; don't just quote words randomly. Does the evidence help explain a metaphor? Does it provide a reason that supports the author's key idea? Does it help show how the author created a certain effect, such as a tone toward the topic or a mood in the reader? Identify this connection clearly for your reader.

What's the Big Idea?

Tracing a Theme

Grade Levels: 6–7; can be adapted up to grade 8 (see note under Overview)

Time Frame: Approximately one class period to get started but extends for two to three weeks as students complete a novel

Overview: The Common Core State Standards for grades 6 and 7 require that students not only *identify* themes but also trace how the themes develop throughout the book. This lesson will teach students to do so. To adapt this lesson up to grade 8, add a step—have students determine a theme, analyze its development over the course of the text, and analyze how the theme relates to the characters, setting, and plot, as outlined in the standards below.

Common Core State Standards

- 6: Reading, Literature, Standard 2: Determine a theme or central idea of a text and how it is conveyed through particular details.

- 6: Reading, Literature, Standard 5: Analyze how a particular sentence, chapter, scene, or stanza fits into the overall structure of a text and contributes to the development of the theme, setting, or plot.

- 7: Reading, Literature, Standard 2: Determine a theme or central idea of a text and analyze its development over the course of the text.

- 8: Reading, Literature, Standard 2: Determine a theme or central idea of a text and analyze its development over the course of the text, including its relationship to the characters, setting, and plot.

- 6–8: Writing, Standard 4: Produce clear and coherent writing in which the development, organization, and style are appropriate to task, purpose, and audience.

Objectives

- Students will identify major themes and ideas in a literary text.

- Students will trace the development of a theme throughout the course of the text.

Background Knowledge Required

Students should be reading a novel or short story in class, but they shouldn't be too far into it. They should be familiar with the word *theme* from earlier grades, although this lesson will review the term and look at it in depth.

Materials Needed

- Copies of novels or short stories

- Notebook paper

Agenda

1. **Introduction**: Write the word *theme* on the board. Have students turn to a partner to define the word and to identify major themes in a recent movie they've seen.

2. **Full-Class Discussion**: Have students share their thoughts. Tell them there is no one right answer. The author does not directly state the theme; students need to read closely to infer what the themes might be. Remind students that a theme is not just presented at the end as an "aha moment" and is not something readers decide on afterward (e.g., that book was about love). A theme is developed *throughout* the course of a movie or book. Have students come up with some examples of how a theme develops throughout the course of a movie. Tell students that they should start thinking about themes early in their reading so they can trace them throughout the course of the book or story.

3. **Independent Work**: Have students take a few minutes to independently jot down possible themes of the texts they are reading. Ask volunteers to share with the full class. Write responses on the board. Pick three themes that the students agree are important.

4. **Wrap-Up**: Tell students to designate three pieces of paper in their notebooks, one for each theme. As they continue to read in class and for homework, they should write down quotes and passages that support each theme. Once students have completed reading their texts, have them choose one of the themes and write an essay about how the author develops it, using evidence from the text. You may wish to review how to incorporate quotations into an essay. See Lesson Plan 15 on page 75 of this book.

Extend the Lesson

- Pair students who wrote on the same themes, and have them compare the evidence they used.

- Have students team up with students who wrote about other themes so they can learn about other perspectives.

Differentiation

For students who need extra support
- Give students some additional sample themes before having them come up with their own.

- Give students guiding questions or prompts to help them trace how a theme is developing.

For advanced students
- You may wish to pair the more advanced students with struggling readers so they can provide prompts and guiding questions on how the author is developing a theme.

Assessment

- Check students' notebook pages for evidence that they have been tracing the themes.

- Use the following rubric (or your own) to assess students' thematic essays. Show students the rubric before they begin writing so they know what will be expected of them.

Additional Resources

- This teacher's lesson provides good examples of text-based strategies for teaching theme: www.brighthubeducation.com/high-school-english-lessons/24132-teaching -theme-using-the-interlopers.

Notes

After implementing the lesson, reflect on what worked and what you would change the next time.

_____

_____

_____

_____

Rubric for Scoring Thematic Essays

	Minimal	Developing	Proficient	Advanced
Content	The student does not pick a theme or picks more than one theme without focusing on one.	The student focuses on a theme but does not support it with evidence from the text or show how it develops.	The student focuses on a theme and includes some evidence from the text to support that theme; evidence might not be sufficient or explained well enough.	The student focuses on one major theme, includes and explains ample evidence from the text to support that theme, and shows how the theme develops.
Organization	Essay lacks a logical organizational pattern.	Essay has some structure but is difficult to follow.	Essay has a logical organizational pattern with a few exceptions.	Essay has a solid introduction and a clear organizational pattern.
Language and Conventions	The errors with language and conventions make the content difficult to understand.	The errors cause confusion for the reader.	There are some errors, but they do not make the content harder to understand.	The student uses language effectively and makes minimal errors in grammar, usage, spelling, and punctuation.

3

Leave Your Opinions for Later!

Producing an Objective Summary

Grade Levels: 6–8

Time Frame: Approximately two class periods

Overview: Middle school students have a hard time understanding the difference between a straightforward summary and a review. This lesson will clarify the differences. You can use this lesson with a literary text as well as with an informational or explanatory one. Coordinate with science and social studies teachers to have students summarize what they're reading in those classes too.

Common Core State Standards

- 6: Reading, Literature, Standard 2: Provide a summary of the text distinct from personal opinions or judgments.

- 7–8: Reading, Literature, Standard 2: Provide an objective summary of the text.

- 6–8: Writing, Standard 4: Produce clear and coherent writing in which the development, organization, and style are appropriate to task, purpose, and audience.

- 6–8: Writing, Standard 6: Use technology, including the Internet, to produce and publish writing . . . as well as to interact and collaborate with others.

Objectives

- Students will compare and contrast the elements of summaries and reviews.

- Students will write objective summaries of a text that demonstrate comprehension.

Background Knowledge Required

Students should have just completed reading a novel or short story in class.

Materials Needed

- Copies of a novel or short story that students have just completed

- Copies of a summary and a review of the same book or movie (found online)

Agenda

1. **Introduction**: Read (or pass out) a summary and a review of a movie to your students. Don't say which is which. Ask students to identify differences between the two texts. Write their responses on the board. Then formally define *summary* and

review. Discuss the word *summary* and its various forms: *summarize, in sum*, etc. Summaries should encompass the main ideas of the whole text and not go off on tangents about specific details. They should not be vague, and they should not outline the entire plot. They should be objective and free of opinions. Point out that a review, on the other hand, does use specific examples but also contains opinions. You may wish to use a Venn diagram on the board so students can see the differences, or have students create their own to review what they've learned.

2. **Modeling**: Pass out some additional examples of good summaries. Ask students to work with partners to identify the ways the authors summed up/expressed the major ideas of the works.

3. **Wrap-Up**: In class or for homework, have students write summaries of a work they have read recently. The next day, you can have students workshop their summaries with partners; partners should provide feedback on objectivity and use of details to support the main idea.

Extend the Lesson

- Have students write reviews of the same novel/short story that they summarized.

- Post students' reviews on a class blog to share with parents or students in other classes, encouraging them to read or not read the work being reviewed.

Differentiation

For students who need extra support
- Have students identify main ideas and details of individual paragraphs and then summarize those paragraphs before they go on to summarize a larger work of literature.

For advanced students
- Have advanced writers help struggling writers understand summaries.

Assessment

- Check students' Venn diagrams for understanding of the differences between the two genres.

- Evaluate students' summaries using the scoring guide on the next page (or an assessment tool of your own choosing).

Additional Resources

- This page provides a list of helpful resources for teaching summarizing: beyondpenguins.ehe.osu.edu/issue/climate-change-and-the-polar-regions/summarizing-and-synthesizing-whats-the-difference.

Notes

After implementing the lesson, reflect on what worked and what you would change the next time.

_____

_____

_____

_____

Scoring Guide for Summaries

Category	Possible Points	Points Earned
The summary focuses on the main idea and includes relevant facts and details.	5	
The summary is well organized and easy to follow.	5	
The summary is written in objective language without opinions or editorializing.	5	
The summary follows the conventions of standard English and contains minimal errors in grammar, usage, spelling, and punctuation.	5	
TOTAL	20	

Who's Telling This Story, Anyway?

Analyzing Narrative Point of View

Lesson Plan 4

Grade Levels: 6–7

Time Frame: Approximately two class periods

Overview: This lesson teaches students how to identify the narrator in a story or novel and to analyze how the author develops the narrative point of view. This lesson shows how to look at the author's use of pronouns to identify the narrator, even when the narrator is an outside observer. The lesson plan can be adapted to any piece of narrative fiction.

Common Core State Standards

- 6: Reading, Literature, Standard 6: Explain how an author develops the point of view of the narrator or speaker in a text.

- 7: Reading, Literature, Standard 6: Analyze how an author develops and contrasts the points of view of different characters or narrators in a text.

- 6–7: Writing, Standard 10: Write routinely over extended time frames (time for research, reflection, and revision) and shorter time frames (a single sitting or a day or two) for a range of discipline-specific tasks, purposes, and audiences.

- 6: Speaking and Listening, Standard 1: Engage effectively in a range of collaborative discussions (one-on-one, in groups, and teacher-led) with diverse partners on *grade 6 topics, texts, and issues*, building on others' ideas and expressing their own clearly.

- 7: Speaking and Listening, Standard 1: Engage effectively in a range of collaborative discussions (one-on-one, in groups, and teacher-led) with diverse partners on *grade 7 topics, texts, and issues*, building on others' ideas and expressing their own clearly.

Objectives

- Students will identify the narrator or speaker in a text.

- Students will understand the difference between the author and the narrator of a text.

- Students will analyze how an author uses pronouns to develop the narrative point of view.

Background Knowledge Required

Students should be reading a novel or short story in class. They should be familiar with the terms *narrator* and *point of view* from earlier grades, although this lesson will review the terms and examine them in depth.

Materials Needed

- Copies of novels or short stories

- Copies of the handout: Narrative Point of View Activity Sheet, p. 21

Agenda

1. **Introduction**: Organize students into two groups. Ask students in Group A to write notes to classmates, telling about something interesting the writer did recently. Students should sign their notes. Ask students in Group B to write notes to classmates, describing something they did this morning (e.g., pack a lunch, board a bus) *from the perspective of an outside observer* (a family member, a family pet, etc.). Have students deliver their notes to the recipients.

   Next, ask a person who received a Group A note to read the note aloud to the class. Ask the class to identify the narrator of the piece. (It should be the student who wrote the note.) Ask the class to identify the point of view of the piece. (It will likely be the first-person point of view.) Then ask a person who received a Group B note to read the note aloud. Ask the class to identify the narrator in this piece. Answering this question will be trickier. Students should recognize that the narrator of this piece is not the person the piece is about; it is an outside observer. Ask the class to identify the point of view of the piece. It most likely will be the third-person point of view. Explain that the narrator of a story or novel is the person who tells what happens. This person may or may not be a character in the story. Whether or not the narrator is in the story helps to determine the point of view.

2. **Activity**: Have students take out the short story or novel they have been reading. Ask them to use the text to complete part 1 of the handout, working in pairs. Then ask volunteers to share responses from their handouts. Use students' responses to clarify or expand on the concepts of narrator and point of view in fiction.

3. **Wrap-Up**: Assign part 2 of the handout for homework. Go over it the next day in class.

Differentiation

For students who need extra support

- Review the cases of personal pronouns so that students understand the difference between first-person and third-person pronouns.

- Ask students to write brief accounts of an event as people who were part of the action, using first-person pronouns. Then have them rewrite the accounts, this time as outside observers, switching to third-person pronouns.

- As students complete part 1 of the handout, assign partners so that more-advanced students can support struggling classmates.

For advanced students

- Collect the notes written by Group A and Group B in the lesson introduction. Ask for volunteers to pull out random notes, read them aloud to the class, and identify the narrators and narrative points of view.

- Use each read aloud as an opportunity to draw the whole class into a discussion of identifying narrators and narrative points of view.

- Repeat as needed to extend the class discussion, helping less advanced students learn from their classmates.

Assessment

Evaluate students' responses on part 2 of the handout, checking to make sure students understand how to identify a narrator and how to analyze an author's use of pronouns to create a narrative point of view.

Additional Resources

- This page provides additional suggestions for teaching narrative point of view as well as a short story, "The House," to use to extend students' practice in identifying a narrator and narrative viewpoint: www.readwritethink.org/classroom-resources/lesson -plans/wolf-analyzing-point-view-23.html.

Notes

After implementing the lesson, reflect on what worked and what you would change next time.

_____

_____

_____

_____

Narrative Point of View Activity Sheet

Part 1: For any story or novel, you can ask a few questions to understand the narrative point of view. Using a work of fiction, answer each of the following questions.

Title of story or novel: _____

Author: _____

Questions	Tips
The Narrator 1. Who is telling what happens? _____ 2. Write down a sentence (or two) from the story that helps you know who is telling what happens. _____ _____ _____	▪ You may or may not know the name of the person telling what happens. If you don't know the name, identify the person with a description. ▪ Look for sentences in which the narrator tells something a character does.
The Narrator's Point of View 3. Is the narrator a character in the story or an outside observer? How do you know? _____ _____ 4. Does the narrator use the first-person point of view or the third-person point of view? How do you know? _____ _____ 5. Whose thoughts does the narrator tell about? Write down a sentence or two from the story as an example. _____ _____ _____	▪ A character in the story takes part in the action and conversations. An outside observer knows what is happening but is not part of the action or conversations. The outside observer often does not have a name or identity; he or she is just the voice telling the story. ▪ Does the narrator tell what happens using first-person pronouns such as *I*, *me*, *we*, and *us*? Or does the narrator tell what happens using mainly third-person pronouns such as *he*, *she*, *they*, and *them*? ▪ A first-person narrator knows only his or her own thoughts. A third-person narrator may know the thoughts of one or more characters.

Part 2: Read each of the following excerpts. Then answer the questions about the narrator and the point of view.

Excerpt A

And so the boy climbed up the tree and gathered her apples and carried them away.
And the tree was happy.

(from *The Giving Tree*, by Shel Silverstein)

1. Who is telling what happens? _____

2. How do you know? _____

3. Whose feelings does the narrator know about? _____

4. What feeling(s) does the narrator reveal? _____

5. Does the narrator use the first-person or the third-person point of view? How do you know?

_____

_____

Excerpt B

"I have a surprise for you," Ruel said, the first time he brought me here. And you know how sick he makes me when he grins.

"What is it?" I asked, not caring in the least.

And that is how we drove up to the house. Four bedrooms and two toilets and a half.

"Isn't it a beauty?" he said, not touching me, but urging me out of the car with the phony enthusiasm in his voice.

(from "Really, *Doesn't* Crime Pay?" by Alice Walker)

6. Who is telling what happens? _____

7. How do you know? _____

8. Whose feelings does the narrator know about? _____

9. What feeling(s) does the narrator reveal? _____

10. Does the narrator use the first-person or third-person point of view? How do you know?

_____

_____

Excerpt C

Back in the room I wrote the boy's temperature down and made a note of the time to give the various capsules.

"Do you want me to read to you?"

"All right. If you want to," said the boy. His face was very white and there were dark areas under his eyes. He lay very still in the bed and seemed very detached from what was going on.

I read aloud from Howard Pyle's *Book of Pirates*; but I could see he was not following what I was reading.

"How do you feel, Schatz?" I asked him.

"Just the same, so far," he said.

. . .

After a while he said to me, "You don't have to stay in here with me Papa, if it bothers you."

"It doesn't bother me."

(from "A Day's Wait," by Ernest Hemingway)

11. Who is telling what happens? _____

12. How do you know? _____

13. Whose feelings does the narrator know about? _____

14. What feeling(s) does the narrator reveal? _____

15. Does the narrator use the first-person or third-person point of view? How do you know?

_____

_____

The Parts vs. the Whole

Studying Informational Text Structures

Grade Levels: 6–7; can be adapted to grade 8 (see note under Overview)

Time Frame: Approximately two class periods

Overview: This lesson is designed to teach students how to examine text structures. The lesson uses the novel *Lord of the Flies* and an article about Maslow's hierarchy of human needs because the two relate. (Pairing informational texts with fiction expands students' depth and perspective.) However, you can use informational articles on any topic for this lesson. To adapt this lesson up to grade 8, don't just look at the major sections of an article; include more on analyzing the role of a particular sentence in developing a key concept.

Common Core State Standards

- 6: Reading, Informational Text, Standard 5: Analyze how a particular sentence, paragraph, chapter, or section fits into the overall structure of a text and contributes to the development of the ideas.

- 7: Reading, Informational Text, Standard 5: Analyze the structure an author uses to organize a text, including how the major sections contribute to the whole and to the development of the ideas.

Objectives

- Students will examine the common organizational structures and features of informational texts.

- Students will compare and contrast ideas from a novel and a related informational article.

Background Knowledge Required

Students should be reading a novel or short story that relates to the informational text you choose to present.

Materials Needed

- Copies of the article about Maslow's hierarchy of human needs: psychology.about.com/od/theoriesofpersonality/a/hierarchyneeds.htm

- Copies of *Lord of the Flies*

- Copies of the handout: Text Structures and Signal Words, p. 27

Agenda

1. **Introduction**: Write *island survival* on the board in big letters. Tell students that today, they'll be thinking about basic needs for survival. Begin with the text (in this case, *Lord of the Flies*). Ask students what needs Piggy and Ralph had when they first arrived on the island. Are they the same things students would need? (If you wish, have students turn to partners and discuss.) Explain that in 1943, a psychologist named Abraham Maslow had a theory of basic human needs.

2. **Full-Group Lesson**: Distribute the article about Maslow. Ask students to preview the article, scanning the layout and features that pop out. What is the title? How is the text broken into different sections? What kinds of visuals are included? How do those elements help readers?

3. **Independent Work**: Have students read the article and jot down notes on how it is organized.

4. **Full-Group Discussion**: Have students share their notes with the full class. Discuss: Does the article use compare and contrast, sequence, problem and solution, description, or a combination of those strategies? How can students tell? Are there any signal words?

5. **Wrap-Up**: Pass out copies of the handout. Ask students to think of sample topics that would benefit from each structure. Go over the handout in class the next day.

Extend the Lesson

- Ask students to write a few paragraphs tying in Maslow's hierarchy to the needs of the characters in *Lord of the Flies*. (The Maslow model is great for understanding character and motivation, as alluded to in reading standard 3.)

Differentiation

For students who need extra support
- Start with an easier informational article or one on an easier topic, such as island survival.

For advanced students
- Give students a more challenging article, possibly one that incorporates more than one kind of organizational method.

Assessment

- Evaluate students' participation in the class discussion to see whether they were able to determine the structure of an informational text and the purpose of the different text features, such as subheads and visuals.

- Check students' work on the handouts to see whether students were able to apply what they learned.

Additional Resources

- Text structure online quizzes and additional handouts are available here: www.ereadingworksheets.com/text-structure.

Notes

After implementing the lesson, reflect on what worked and what you would change the next time.

_____

_____

_____

_____

Name: _____   Date: _____

Text Structures and Signal Words

The following table describes different ways an author may organize an informational text. It also shows the signal words you can look for to determine the kind of text structure being used. Read the first two columns, and then complete the column on the far right.

Text Structure	Common Signal Words and Phrases	An Author Might Use This Structure to Explain . . .
compare/contrast	*however, on the other hand, similarly, as opposed to, like, unlike, although, both*	
problem/solution	*as a result, the reason that, the proposal to, concluded that*	
time order (sequence)	*first, second, then, next, last, finally, before, after*	
cause/effect	*because, as a result, due to, consequently*	
description	*for example, for instance, such as, also, in addition*	

Did That *Really* Happen?

Examining Fact and Fiction in Historical Texts

Grade Levels: 6–7

Time Frame: Approximately two class periods

Overview: In this lesson, students will read a fictional account and a historical account of the same event. This lesson uses "Crispus Attucks: Martyr for American Independence," by Langston Hughes, and a more straightforward biography of Attucks from Biography.com. You could use another text pairing instead. Another suggestion is *Wild Ginger*, by Anchee Min, a novel about the Cultural Revolution in China, compared to a textbook or an encyclopedia article, or Nien Cheng's personal account of that time, *Life and Death in Shanghai* (1987), compared to the textbook article. You may wish to coordinate with the social studies teacher and choose texts related to what students are learning in that class.

Note that this lesson applies to grades 6 and 7, which have similar standards on comparing different genres (in grade 6, two genres of your choice; in grade 7, a fictional and historical account of the same period). In grade 8, the standard changes; the emphasis turns to analyzing how a modern work of fiction draws on themes, patterns of events, or character types from myths, traditional stories, or religious works.

Common Core State Standards

- 6: Reading, Literature, Standard 9: Compare and contrast texts in different forms or genres . . . in terms of their approaches to similar themes and topics.

- 7: Reading, Literature, Standard 9: Compare and contrast a fictional portrayal of a time, place, or character and a historical account of the same period as a means of understanding how authors of fiction use or alter history.

- 6–7: Reading, Literature, Standard 4: Determine the meanings of words and phrases as they are used in a text, including figurative and connotative meanings.

- 6–7: Writing, Standard 10: Write routinely over extended time frames . . . and shorter time frames . . . for a range of discipline-specific tasks, purposes, and audiences.

Objectives

- Students will compare and contrast two versions of the same event in history.

- Students will explore the reasons that a reader might choose one kind of text over another when wanting to learn more about an event.

Background Knowledge Required

Familiarity with the American Revolution, particularly the Boston Massacre, would be helpful but is not necessary.

Materials Needed

- Copies of "Crispus Attucks: Martyr for American Independence," found at Google Books: tinyurl.com/7h2pz85

- Copies of the biography of Crispus Attucks from Biography.com: www.biography .com/people/crispus-attucks-9191864

Agenda

1. **Introduction**: Ask students if they've seen a movie or TV show that was *based* on true events but that altered the true story a little. Why might directors or screenwriters alter real-life events? Jot down students' responses on the board. Tell them that today, they're going to compare a fictionalized and historical version of the same event.

2. **Full-Class Activity**: Distribute "Crispus Attucks." Read slowly as a class for comprehension. Then read the Biography.com article. Ask students how the two accounts differ. Draw a Venn diagram on the board and ask students for input. Ask them to consider language, facts, tone, what's included and what's omitted, and so on.

3. **Wrap-Up**: Have students write paragraphs summarizing how Hughes's account is a more literary take on a historical event and why a reader might prefer one version or the other. You may wish to provide sentence frames that use the language of comparison: *while, but, however*, etc.

Extend the Lesson

- Have students write their own versions of an event from history. They should create one- or two-paragraph encyclopedia entries and one- or two-page fictionalized versions.

Differentiation

For students who need extra support

- Use an excerpt from "Crispus Attucks" rather than the whole piece so you can spend more time making sure students understand it.

For advanced students

- Have students share their responses with the full class so the struggling writers will see models of effective comparison writing.

- Have advanced students read a third account about Crispus Attucks or even see a visual about him to compare to the texts. Advanced students may be able to read this interesting article: "When is Fiction as Good as Fact? Comparing the Influence of Documentary and Historical Reenactment Films on Engagement, Affect, Issue Interest, and Learning," at academic.csuohio.edu/kneuendorf/c32111/LaMarre %26Landreville09.pdf.

Assessment

- Evaluate whether students were able to identify the differences between the two texts, as evidenced by their participation during the class discussion.

- Assess students' paragraphs on Hughes's literary take versus the straightforward historical account and the benefits and drawbacks of both versions.

Additional Resources

- This page from ReadWriteThink has a clear definition of historical fiction: www .readwritethink.org/files/resources/lesson_images/lesson404/HistoricalFictionDefn .pdf.

Notes

After implementing the lesson, reflect on what worked and what you would change the next time.

_____

_____

_____

_____

See It, Hear It, Love It (or Hate It)!

Compare Print and Audio Versions of a Poem

Grade Levels: 6–7; can be adapted to grade 8 (see note under Overview)

Time Frame: Approximately two class periods

Overview: In this lesson, students will compare the text of "The Road Not Taken" to an audio version read by the author, Robert Frost, to discover the effects different mediums have on readers or listeners. "The Road Not Taken" was chosen as the sample text because it's a complex yet accessible text. If you wish, you can do this lesson with a different poem.

Note that this lesson focuses on grades 6 and 7, which have similar standards about comparing a written text with a filmed or recorded version. In grade 8, the standard changes and focuses on whether the recorded version is faithful to or departs from the text or script. To adapt this lesson up to grade 8, choose a play or novel that has been performed and spend time on whether the actors' and director's decisions seem to be faithful to the original work.

Common Core State Standards

- 6: Reading, Literature, Standard 7: Compare and contrast the experience of reading a story, drama, or poem to listening to or viewing an audio, video, or live version of the text, including contrasting what students "see" and "hear" when reading the text to what they perceive when they listen or watch.

- 7: Reading, Literature, Standard 7: Compare and contrast a written story, drama, or poem to its audio, filmed, staged, or multimedia version, analyzing the effects of techniques unique to each medium (e.g., lighting, sound, color, or camera focus and angles in a film).

- 6–7: Writing, Standard 2: Write informative/explanatory texts to examine a topic and convey ideas, concepts, and information through the selection, organization, and analysis of relevant content.

- 6–7: Writing, Standard 9: Draw evidence from literary or informational texts to support analysis, reflection, and research.

- 6–7: Speaking and Listening, Standard 1: Engage effectively in a range of collaborative discussions . . . with diverse partners *on [grades 6–7] topics, texts, and issues,* building on others' ideas and expressing their own clearly.

Objectives

- Students will compare and contrast the written and audio versions of a poem, paying close attention to what they "see" and "hear" in each version.

Background Knowledge Required

No particular background knowledge is required for this lesson.

Materials Needed

- A copy of "The Road Not Taken" for each student, preferably copies that students can mark up. The poem is available from the Poetry Foundation: www.poetryfoundation .org/poem/173536.

- An audio recording of the poem is available here: www.poets.org/viewmedia.php/ prmMID/15717

Agenda

1. **Introduction**: Draw a large Venn diagram on the board, labeling one side "Written" and the other side "Audio." Label the entire diagram "The Road Not Taken." Tell students that they will compare and contrast the written and audio versions of Robert Frost's poem.

2. **Think-Pair-Share**: Ask students to silently read the poem. Encourage them to read it a second time so they can begin to dig into its meaning and their personal responses to it. Have students write responses to such sentence starters as "In my mind's eye, I see . . ." and "With my mind's ear, I hear . . . " They should note or tag lines or phrases from the poem that correspond to their responses. Next, pair students to compare and discuss their written responses. Finally, initiate a full-class discussion by asking students to respond to a spoken prompt, such as "Tell me about your experience of reading 'The Road Not Taken.'"

3. **Full-Class Activity**: Have students listen to the audio version and take notes on what they "see" and hear during this experience. Play the audio version a second time, encouraging students to add to their first-impression notes. Then ask students to help you fill in the Venn diagram on the board, comparing and contrasting their impressions of the written and audio versions. Students should take notes on their own Venn diagrams. Make sure that students use examples from the audio version to support their ideas.

4. **Wrap-Up**: For homework, have students write brief essays comparing and contrasting the written and audio versions of the poem. Ask them to focus on the strengths and weaknesses of each version.

Extend the Lesson

- Have students create their own audio reading of the poem and post it on a class website or an online site such as YouTube.

Differentiation

For students who need extra support

- Provide a list of possible elements to examine while reading and listening to the poem. Examples for the silent reading include descriptive words, emotional language, rhyme, theme, and narrative point of view. Examples for the audio experience can include the previous list plus elements such as emphasis placed on words, pace (speed) of reading, tone of voice, the mood created in readers, speaker's regional accent, and so on.

For advanced students

- Engage advanced students during a full-class discussion to form lists of elements to examine during the silent and audio readings of the poem, as described in the bullet above. A good time to do this may be *between* the first and second silent readings and between the first and second audio readings.

Assessment

- Evaluate students' written notes and tags from the think-pair-share activity, checking to make sure they noted details about what they "saw" *and* "heard" during their reading of the poem.

- Before assigning homework, evaluate students' Venn diagrams to see whether students noted two or three elements in each section of the diagram, supportable by details and examples from the written *and* audio versions of the poem.

- Use the following rubric to evaluate students' essays.

Score 4.0	The student • Identifies at least two similarities between the written and audio versions of the poem, using examples from BOTH texts. • Identifies at least two differences between the written and audio versions of the poem, using examples from BOTH texts. • Identifies at least one strength and one weakness of each version. No major errors or omissions in the score 4.0 content.
Score 3.5	The student demonstrates success at the 3.0 level plus partial success at the 4.0 level.
Score 3.0	The student • Identifies one similarity between the written and audio versions of the poem, using examples from BOTH texts. • Identifies one difference between the written and audio versions of the poem, using examples from BOTH texts. • Identifies one strength and one weakness of one version OR one strength or weakness from each version. No major errors or omissions in the score 3.0 content.
Score 2.5	The student demonstrates success at the 2.0 level plus partial success at the 3.0 level.

Score 2.0	The student • Identifies one similarity between the written and audio versions of the poem. • Identifies one difference between the written and audio versions of the poem. • Identifies a strength or weakness of one of the versions. No major errors or omissions in the score 2.0 content.
Score 1.5	The student demonstrates partial success at the 2.0 level; responses may be overly simplistic or limited.
Score 1.0	With help, the student achieves partial success at score 2.0 and 3.0 contents; responses are simplistic and limited.
Score 0.5	With help, the student achieves partial success at score 2.0 content but not score 3.0 content.
Score 0.0	Even with help, the student has no success.

Additional Resources

Here are additional text-audio pairs that will work effectively for this lesson. You can find even more at Poets.org: www.poets.org/page.php/prmID/361.

- "The Junior High School Band Concert," by David Wagoner: www.poets.org/viewmedia.php/prmMID/15383

- "The Negro Speaks of Rivers," by Langston Hughes: www.poets.org/viewmedia.php/prmMID/15722

Notes

After implementing the lesson, reflect on what worked and what you would change the next time.

_____

_____

_____

_____

Everyone's Entitled to an Opinion

Determine the Author's Point of View

Lesson Plan 8

Grade Levels: 7– 8; can be adapted to grade 6 (see note under Overview)

Time Frame: Approximately one or two class periods

Overview: This lesson teaches students how to determine an author's point of view in an opinion or argumentative text. It also teaches students how to analyze the way the author acknowledges and responds to conflicting evidence or viewpoints. The lesson can be adapted for grade 6 by omitting the sections on opposing viewpoints.

Common Core State Standards
- 7: Reading, Informational Text, Standard 6: Determine an author's point of view or purpose in a text and analyze how the author distinguishes his or her own position from that of others.

- 8: Reading, Informational Text, Standard 6: Determine an author's point of view or purpose in a text and analyze how the author acknowledges and responds to conflicting evidence or viewpoints.

- 7–8: Language, Standard 6: Acquire and accurately use grade-appropriate general academic and domain-specific words and phrases; gather vocabulary knowledge when considering a word or phrase important to comprehension or expression.

Objectives
- Students will identify an author's point of view in an opinion or argumentative text.

- Students will analyze how an author responds to opposing viewpoints.

- Students will accurately use the terms *argument, point of view, fact, opinion,* and *evidence.*

Background Knowledge Required
Students should be familiar with the term *point of view* from earlier grades, but the term will be reviewed in this lesson. Through grade 5, the Common Core State Standards use the term *opinion piece* in conjunction with discussion of text types; now, in middle school, the Common Core uses the term *argument* instead.

Materials Needed
- Copies of "Selling Candy to Kids" at www.nytimes.com/2011/11/19/opinion/selling -candy-to-kids.html. If you prefer, you can pair up with a social studies or science

teacher and choose a different article based on what students are studying in those classes.

- Copies of the handout: Let's Talk About Argumentative Texts!, p. 39

Agenda

1. **Introduction**: Ask each student to draw a line on a sheet of paper, dividing it into two columns. Students should label one column "Five Healthful Foods I Should Eat (but Don't)" and label the other column "Five Junk Foods I Eat (but Shouldn't)." Give students a few minutes to fill in the columns; meanwhile, create an empty master chart on the board. Ask volunteers to name items from their lists. Fill in the master chart with student responses. As you do so, ask students about their points of view on healthful and unhealthful foods. For example, "From your point of view, what makes this food healthful or unhealthful?" and "In your opinion, would this food be a smart choice for the school lunch menu? Why or why not?" Explain that many people and groups, from parents to corporations to the government, have strong points of view about what young people should or should not eat. Remind students that a point of view is an opinion, or belief, about a topic. Different people can have different points of view on the same topic.

2. **Think-Pair-Share**: Pass out copies of "Selling Candy to Kids." Ask students to read the article independently and to underline and label one fact and one opinion in the piece. Meanwhile, create a two-column chart on the board, labeling the columns "Facts" and "Opinions." Next, pair students and have them share ideas about facts and opinions in the article. Finally, ask the pairs to contribute their ideas in a class discussion. Fill in the master chart with students' contributions of facts and opinions. Ask questions such as "Why is this statement a fact and not an opinion?" and "How do you know this is an opinion and not a fact?" If students are having trouble distinguishing facts from opinions, review the terms on the handout.

3. **Lesson**: Explain that writers of opinion and argument pieces use facts as evidence to support their points of view. Ask students to use information in the facts/opinions chart, in conjunction with the article, to help them identify the writer's point of view in "Selling Candy to Kids." Struggling students may suggest "Candy is bad" or "No one should advertise candy to kids." Stronger responses may include "We need legal guidelines, not voluntary guidelines, for ads for junk food aimed at kids." Students may point to the article's closing sentence as a strong statement of the author's point of view: "Instead of giving in to lobbyists, the Obama administration should be doing more to limit the way unhealthy foods are sold to children." Review key terms, such as *point of view*, on the handout as needed.

    Explain that strong arguments include facts, or evidence, to support an author's point of view. Tell students that writers often take their arguments a step further by pointing out opposing viewpoints and then showing those viewpoints to be weak or wrong. Ask students to examine "Selling Candy to Kids" and look for examples of opposing viewpoints. The strongest examples are the two statements in the next-to-last paragraph. Point out that the author used most of the article to explain his point of view. The opposing viewpoints are included as quick statements, and then a long final paragraph shows the opposing viewpoints to be weak. The closing paragraph also restates the writer's main point of view on selling candy to kids.

4. **Wrap-Up**: Give students an additional argumentative text to read for homework. After reading the article, they should do three things:

   a. Create facts/opinions charts.
   b. Write one-paragraph summaries of the writer's point of view.
   c. Identify one example of an opposing viewpoint in the article and how the author shows it to be weak or wrong.

Differentiation

For students who need extra support

- Remind students that the title of a piece often identifies the topic of the piece. Sometimes the title states the writer's point of view. Often, the final paragraph states or restates the writer's point of view.

- Use the handout to review academic vocabulary related to analyzing arguments. Pair advanced students with struggling students and ask them to complete the handout, using either "Selling Candy to Kids" or the article selected for the wrap-up activity.

For advanced students

- Offer students the option of completing the wrap-up activity using an argumentative text of their own choosing. The editorial section of a local newspaper or a national newspaper such as the *New York Times*, *USA Today*, or the *Washington Post* is a good place to look. Students should turn in a copy of the article with their work.

Assessment

- Grade students' work on the handout. The handout can be used once in class during the lesson as a teaching tool, and a fresh copy can be used as part of the wrap-up activity.

- Use the following rubric to assess students' work in the wrap-up activity.

Score 4.0	The student • Identifies facts and opinions in the article. • Identifies the writer's point of view in the article. • Identifies one opposing viewpoint and the writer's response to it. No major errors or omissions in the score 4.0 content.
Score 3.5	The student demonstrates success at the 3.0 level plus partial success at the 4.0 level.
Score 3.0	The student • Identifies facts and opinions in the article. • Identifies the writer's point of view in the article. No major errors or omissions in the score 3.0 content.
Score 2.5	The student demonstrates success at the 2.0 level plus partial success at the 3.0 level.

Score 2.0	The student
	▪ Identifies facts and opinions in the article.
	OR
	▪ Identifies the writer's point of view in the article.
	No major errors or omissions in the score 2.0 content.
Score 1.5	The student demonstrates partial success at the 2.0 level; responses may be overly simplistic or limited.
Score 1.0	With help, the student achieves partial success at score 2.0 and 3.0 contents; responses are simplistic and limited.
Score 0.5	With help, the student achieves partial success at score 2.0 content but not score 3.0 content.
Score 0.0	Even with help, the student has no success.

Additional Resources

Here are additional argumentative texts to use in the wrap-up and differentiation activities:

- "Bullying in School," by CarrieAnn13: www.teenink.com/opinion/school_college/article/331645/Bullying-in-School. Use this article with struggling students.

- "'Homework Trap' Is a Difficult Challenge for Students, Parents and Educators," by Kenneth Goldberg: www.nj.com/times-opinion/index.ssf/2012/05/opinion_homework_trap_is_a_dif.html. Use this article with more advanced students.

Notes

After implementing the lesson, reflect on what worked and what you would change next time.

_____

_____

_____

_____

Let's Talk About Argumentative Texts!

A Glossary of Academic Vocabulary

argument   an organized expression of a person's point of view on a topic, including evidence to support the viewpoint, recognition of at least one opposing viewpoint, and, often, a rebuttal (argument against) the opposing viewpoint. An argument goes a step further than an opinion piece by noting and arguing against opposing viewpoints.

Write down the title of a text that that presents an argument:

1. _____

_____

evidence   the facts, examples, and reasons that an author uses to try to persuade readers to agree with his or her point of view on a topic

Write down two pieces of evidence that an author uses to support his or her viewpoint in an argument:

2. _____

3. _____

fact   a statement that can be proven true. Fact statements often use numbers, as in "Fifty-four percent of the students in Ferndale Middle School are female." Fact statements often use proper nouns, as in "In 2011, the Federal Trade Commission considered creating voluntary nutritional standards for foods marketed to children."

Write down two facts that an author uses in an argument:

4. _____

5. _____

opinion   a statement of a personal idea, belief, or point of view. Opinions are arguable, meaning that people disagree over them. No one would argue that dogs are pets (this is a statement of fact), but people do argue over whether dogs make the *best* pets (this is an opinion). Opinions often use judgment words such as *better, best, beautiful, boring, valuable,* and so on.

Write down two opinions that an author uses in an argument:

6. _____

7. _____

point of view (also viewpoint)   In an argument or opinion text, the author's point of view is his or her way of looking at the topic. The point of view is an opinion that the author seeks to support with *evidence*, or facts and convincing statements.

Write down an author's point of view in an argument:

8. _____

_____

_____

You Be the Judge

*Determining Whether the Evidence Is
Sound, Sufficient, and Relevant*

Grade Levels: 7–8; can be adapted down to grade 6 (see note under Overview)

Time Frame: Approximately one class period

Overview: In this lesson, students analyze the evidence presented in an informational text. They will decide whether the author has provided enough logical, relevant evidence to support his or her claims. To adapt this lesson down to grade 6, have students identify which claims are supported by evidence and which claims are not. Omit the section on whether the evidence is relevant, logical, and sufficient.

Common Core State Standards

- 7: Reading, Informational Text, Standard 8: Trace and evaluate the argument and specific claims in a text, assessing whether the reasoning is sound and the evidence is relevant and sufficient to support the claims.

- 8: Reading, Informational Text, Standard 8: Delineate and evaluate the argument and specific claims in a text, assessing whether the reasoning is sound and the evidence is relevant and sufficient; recognize when irrelevant evidence is introduced.

Objectives

- Students will identify the claims made by the authors of informational articles.

- Students will evaluate whether the claims are supported by sufficient, relevant, logical evidence.

Background Knowledge Required

No particular knowledge is required for this lesson.

Materials Needed

- Copies of four short *New York Times* opinion articles—"Behind Bars, Teenagers Become Prey"; "Prison Does Not Make Good Citizens"; "In Sentencing, Remember the Victims"; and "Adult Punishments Should Be an Option"—from the Room for Debate page reflecting each side of the issue about whether juvenile offenders should be sent to prison: www.nytimes.com/roomfordebate/2012/06/05/when-to-punish-a-young-offender-and-when-to-rehabilitate

    Note that this topic was chosen because it is current and relevant to teens; however, violence and sexuality are mentioned in these articles. You may choose a different topic depending on the maturity of your students and your own judgment. This lesson can be done with other kinds of informational texts such as literary nonfiction.

- Copies of the handout: Evaluating an Argument, p. 44

Agenda

1. **Introduction**: Put two sample statements on the board, and ask students which is more convincing and why.

   > Teens who commit crimes should be sent to rehabilitation, not prison, because rehabilitation will help them learn right from wrong and teach them to be more responsible in the future. Prison won't teach them anything, because they'll be forced to live with other criminals. A 2010 study from the Teen Life Institute* showed that teens who emerge from rehabilitation are better able to adjust to society than those who were imprisoned.

   > Teens who commit crimes should be sent to rehabilitation, not prison. Rehabilitation centers are nice places, and a lot of caring counselors work there. There are rehabilitation centers all over the country. Prisons are often frightening and dangerous places. A lot of fights take place in prison cafeterias. Prisoners are often lonely and do not get many visits from family members and friends.

   (*Note that the statistic and agency were made up for the purpose of this example.) Discuss as a class. Explain that in the second statement, connections are missing. The author does not explain what the conditions at the rehabilitation center or in prison have to do with juvenile offenders' lives. Tell students that when writing and reading an argument, evidence must be relevant. It must also be sound and sufficient. Discuss what those three terms mean.

2. **Partner Activity**: Pass out the *New York Times* articles, and have students work in pairs. Half the pairs get the pro side and half get the con side. Students work with partners to annotate the two texts on their side by carefully examining each claim made by an author and evaluating whether it is sound, sufficient, and relevant. Students can use the handout to take notes.

3. **Wrap-Up**: When students are done, have them decide which of the two articles presents a stronger argument. Have them share with the class so that students on the other side can learn another perspective.

Extend the Lesson

- Have students evaluate the arguments made by some of the *New York Times* readers who submitted comments on the articles. You may also wish to apply this lesson to students' argumentative writing. See Writing Lesson Plan 20 on page 92 of this book.

Differentiation

For students who need extra support

- Make sure students understand the authors' claims before moving on to evaluating the evidence used.

For advanced students

- You may wish to pair students by reading level so that the advanced students can read higher-level articles.

Assessment

- Evaluate students' work on the handout.

- You can also have students write short reflections on what they learned during the lesson.

Additional Resources

- This page provides a list of helpful questions to ask when evaluating an argument: academic.cuesta.edu/acasupp/as/403.htm.

Notes

After implementing the lesson, reflect on what worked and what you would change the next time.

_____

_____

_____

_____

Evaluating an Argument

Claim	Evidence presented to support that claim	Is the evidence sound, sufficient, and relevant? Explain.

Is a Picture Worth a Thousand Words?

How Different Mediums Explain an Idea

Grade Levels: 6–8

Time Frame: Approximately two class periods

Overview: In this lesson, students will examine Dorothea Lange's photography about the dust bowl and compare it to historical accounts about that period. You could also do this lesson using visuals and text about another historical event. For example, you could show students photographs of the "lost boys" of Sudan and compare them with interviews with these men. You could also choose a recent news event and discuss how photos in news magazines affect readers differently than the accompanying text does. You may wish to coordinate with a social studies teacher on this lesson.

Common Core State Standards

- 6: Reading, Informational Text, Standard 7: Integrate information presented in different media or formats . . . as well as in words to develop a coherent understanding of a topic or issue.

- 7: Reading, Informational Text, Standard 7: Compare and contrast a text to an audio, a video, or a multimedia version of the text, analyzing each medium's portrayal of the subject.

- 8: Reading, Informational Text, Standard 7: Evaluate the advantages and disadvantages of using different mediums (e.g., print or digital text, video, multimedia) to present a particular topic or idea.

- 6–8: Writing, Standard 10: Write routinely over extended time frames . . . and shorter time frames . . . for a range of discipline-specific tasks, purposes, and audiences.

- 6–8: Speaking and Listening, Standard 1: Engage effectively in a range of collaborative discussions . . . with diverse partners on *[grades 6–8] topics, texts, and issues,* building on others' ideas and expressing their own clearly.

Objectives

- Students will evaluate the purposes and benefits of different mediums to convey ideas.

- Students will analyze photographs and consider how they provide meaning and emotion that is not provided in a text on the same topic.

Background Knowledge Required

No particular knowledge is required for this lesson.

Materials Needed

- Dorothea Lange photographs, found on websites such as this one: www.historyplace.com/unitedstates/lange/index.html

- Copies of a concise summary of the dust bowl: www.ncdc.noaa.gov/paleo/drought/drght_history.html

- If time permits, this PBS documentary on the dust bowl: www.pbs.org/wgbh/americanexperience/films/dustbowl

Agenda

1. **Introduction**: Write *photos*, *text*, and *videos* on the board in big letters. Give students a variety of situations, such as "teaching a sixth grader about the American Revolution" or "getting people to donate money to a charity." Ask students which form would be best for accomplishing each goal. Students might say that more than one form is appropriate; they should explain why. What are the benefits and drawbacks of each form?

2. **Full-Class Activity**: Have students read the summary of the dust bowl.

3. **Group Work**: Organize students into small groups of three or four. Give each group a couple of photos by Dorothea Lange. Have students do close "readings" of the photos, describing in their own words what might be happening and what the subjects might be thinking and feeling. Students should identify details in the photos as well as lighting and camera angles. You might also have students generate a list of words each photo evokes and later see whether those words appear in the written texts.

4. **Full-Class Activity**: Have groups share with the full class. If each group has different photos to work with, it would be helpful to display larger versions on the board or pass them around so the other groups can see them.

5. **Wrap-Up**: In class or for homework, have students write brief paragraphs about how the photos enhanced their understanding of or reactions to what they learned about the dust bowl from the texts.

Extend the Lesson

- Show the documentary on the dust bowl and discuss how it adds to students' understanding of the period.

- This lesson covered photography. You could continue the discussion about different genres by displaying paintings of the dust bowl or another topic. You might have students compare Longfellow's poem about Paul Revere to the Revere painting by Grant Wood. Painting: http://tinyurl.com/cv35ufy. Text: www.bartleby.com/42/789.html.

- Have students read the Leonardo da Vinci essay "Painting is superior to poetry": www.fromoldbooks.org/Richter-NotebooksOfLeonardo/section-8/item-654.html. Have students summarize da Vinci's points and then debate whether they agree or disagree.

- Consider pairing this lesson with an excerpt from *The Grapes of Wrath*. Students can read letters from survivors of the dust bowl and explore how they compare to the text and the photographs. They can also write letters from the perspective of the people in the photos.

Differentiation

For students who need extra support
- Provide students with extra vocabulary and comprehension support as they read the article on the dust bowl.

For advanced students
- Students can read higher-level texts about the dust bowl.

Assessment

- Evaluate students' participation during the class discussion to see whether they thought critically about the differences between photography and text and how they conveyed meaning and feeling.

- Check students' paragraphs for evidence of understanding.

Additional Resources

- This Library of Congress guide offers ways to teach students to analyze photographs and prints: www.loc.gov/teachers/usingprimarysources/resources/Analyzing _Photographs_and_Prints.pdf.

Notes

After implementing the lesson, reflect on what worked and what you would change the next time.

_____

_____

_____

_____

# These Authors Aren't on the Same Page

Analyze Texts with Conflicting Information

Lesson Plan 11

Grade Levels: 7–8; can be adapted down to grade 6 (see note in Overview)

Time Frame: Approximately one or two class periods

Overview: In this lesson, students will examine conflicting interpretations of the actions of General William T. Sherman from the American Civil War. This social studies topic was chosen because the Common Core encourages content collaboration across disciplines. You may wish to coordinate with a social studies or science teacher to choose readings about a person, an event, or a natural phenomenon that have conflicting information or differing interpretations.

Note that this lesson is for grades 7 and 8. To adapt it down to grade 6, focus on having students compare and contrast two authors' presentations of events. You don't have to go as deeply with having students analyze conflicting information or look at how authors emphasize different information.

Common Core State Standards

- 7: Reading, Informational Text, Standard 9: Analyze how two or more authors writing about the same topic shape their presentations of key information by emphasizing different evidence or advancing different interpretations of facts.

- 8: Reading, Informational Text, Standard 9: Analyze a case in which two or more texts provide conflicting information on the same topic and identify where the texts disagree on matters of fact or interpretation.

- 7–8: Writing, Standard 1: Write arguments to support claims with clear reasons and relevant evidence.

- 7–8: Writing, Standard 9: Draw evidence from literary or informational texts to support analysis, reflection, and research.

- 7: Speaking and Listening, Standard 1: Engage effectively in a range of collaborative discussions . . . with diverse partners on *grade 7 topics, texts, and issues*, building on others' ideas and expressing their own clearly.

- 8: Speaking and Listening, Standard 1: Engage effectively in a range of collaborative discussions . . . with diverse partners on *grade 8 topics, texts, and issues*, building on others' ideas and expressing their own clearly.

Objectives

- Students will read two texts that discuss the same topic but interpret the facts differently.

- Students will analyze how writers use words, phrases, and sentences to shape their presentations of key information, creating differing or conflicting accounts of a given topic.

Background Knowledge Required

Students should be familiar with the difference between a fact and an opinion. You may want to tell students that when people interpret facts or draw conclusions from facts, they often are forming opinions.

Materials Needed

- Copies of "William Tecumseh Sherman" from History.com: www.history.com/topics/william-t-sherman

- Copies of "Forefather/villain" from the *Pittsburgh Post-Gazette*: www.post-gazette.com/stories/opinion/david-shribman/forefathervillain-479952

Agenda

1. **Introduction**: Write the following prompt on the board: "You arrive at a big party at a friend's house. Things go OK at first, but then people start to get a little wild. You realize that no adults are on the premises. You step outside and send two texts, one to your parent/guardian and one to a friend who is not at the party. What do your texts say?" Ask students to jot down their texts. Then ask volunteers to read their texts aloud to the class. Use the texts as points of reference to discuss how people can interpret facts in different ways for different purposes.

2. **Activity**: Pass out copies of the two articles. Organize students into Group A and Group B. Ask Group A to read "William Tecumseh Sherman," focusing on paragraphs six, seven, and eight. Ask Group B to read "Forefather/villain," focusing on paragraphs four, five, six, 11, 12, and 13. As they read, students should mark words, phrases, and sentences that show Sherman in either a positive or a negative light. Next, organize students into small groups within their larger groups. Ask them to compare and analyze their findings from the reading activity.

3. **Full-Class Activity**: Draw a T-chart on the board, labeling one side "Hero" and the other side "Villain." Label the entire chart "William T. Sherman." Ask students to help you fill in the chart with specific words, phrases, and sentences from the reading activity. Explain that there is a factual record of Sherman's actions, but people interpret those facts in different ways. Students should create T-charts on their own paper and take notes.

   Remind students of the opening activity in which they wrote two different texts about the same wild party. How did they interpret the facts to create two different impressions of the party? In the same way, accounts of people, events, and natural phenomena can be shaped in different ways by emphasizing different evidence and interpreting facts in different ways.

4. **Wrap-Up**: For homework, ask students to write letters to the LSU Board of Supervisors either in support of or in opposition to naming a building on the LSU campus after Sherman. Students should use at least three reasons or examples from one or both texts to support their viewpoints.

Extend the Lesson

- Ask students to work with partners to prepare five-minute oral presentations answering this question: How can two authors write about the same topic but shape their presentations of key information differently? Students can use evidence from the two articles on Sherman to explain their ideas.

- Advanced students might use evidence from articles on a different topic, such as climate change (truth or hoax?) or Benedict Arnold (hero or villain?).

Differentiation

For students who need extra support

- Assign students to Group A or B in advance, and give them the articles to read ahead of time. Ask them to come to class prepared to answer this question: "Does this article show Sherman to be mostly a hero or mostly a villain?"

For advanced students

- Give students the option of reading both articles in advance, regardless of which group they are in. Ask them to come to class prepared to answer this question: "How can one person be both a hero and a villain?" Include an advanced student in each small discussion group, assigning him or her to be the group scribe, someone who, during discussion, creates a master list of the group's ideas and prompts individuals to contribute thoughts.

Assessment

- Listen in during the small-group discussions, pointing out when students are doing a good job of linking words, phrases, and sentences in the text to their ideas and helping struggling students find appropriate evidence.

- Review students' T-charts, checking to see that they included at least three examples on each side of the chart.

- Use the following rubric to evaluate the letters that students wrote for the wrap-up activity.

Score 4.0	The student
	- Writes using a letter format, addressing the letter to the LSU Board of Supervisors.
	- Takes a clear stand for or against naming a building on the LSU campus after William T. Sherman.
	- Identifies at least three reasons, drawn from one or both texts, in support of his or her point of view.
	No major errors or omissions in the score 4.0 content.

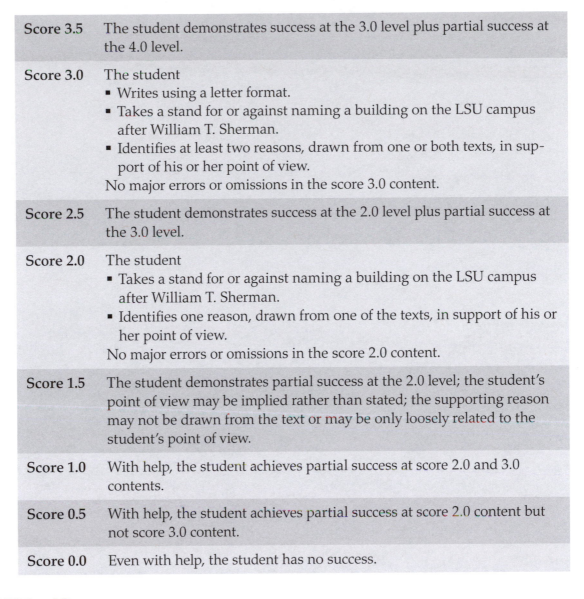

Score 3.5	The student demonstrates success at the 3.0 level plus partial success at the 4.0 level.
Score 3.0	The student • Writes using a letter format. • Takes a stand for or against naming a building on the LSU campus after William T. Sherman. • Identifies at least two reasons, drawn from one or both texts, in support of his or her point of view. No major errors or omissions in the score 3.0 content.
Score 2.5	The student demonstrates success at the 2.0 level plus partial success at the 3.0 level.
Score 2.0	The student • Takes a stand for or against naming a building on the LSU campus after William T. Sherman. • Identifies one reason, drawn from one of the texts, in support of his or her point of view. No major errors or omissions in the score 2.0 content.
Score 1.5	The student demonstrates partial success at the 2.0 level; the student's point of view may be implied rather than stated; the supporting reason may not be drawn from the text or may be only loosely related to the student's point of view.
Score 1.0	With help, the student achieves partial success at score 2.0 and 3.0 contents.
Score 0.5	With help, the student achieves partial success at score 2.0 content but not score 3.0 content.
Score 0.0	Even with help, the student has no success.

Additional Resources

- Additional ideas for teaching two or more texts with conflicting information or interpretations are in Brooke Anderson's blog post: edublahg.blogspot.com/2011/11/how-to-teach-common-core-english-8.html.

Notes

After implementing the lesson, reflect on what worked and what you would change next time.

Writing

Part 2

Overview

The Common Core's writing standards won't change the basic way you teach writing—through prewriting, drafting, revising, and editing. However, they might lead to changes in the genres you cover. If you haven't been doing so already, make sure you spend plenty of time on argument and informational writing. Those genres require that students use evidence from a variety of sources. Devote time to teaching students how to conduct research, how to evaluate their sources for reliability and credibility, and how to incorporate sources effectively. Those are crucial skills for students to have in college and beyond. Also try to incorporate technology into the writing process. The standards require that students use technology to produce and publish writing. The list below provides additional guidelines for revising your current writing lessons or for creating new ones.

Planning Checklist

When planning a CCSS-based writing lesson, remember these tips:

☐ If you don't already spend a lot of time on argument and informative writing, make them a bigger part of your curriculum. In the middle and high school standards, there is a decreased emphasis on narrative writing and an increased focus on argument and informative writing.

☐ Show students that genres often merge—for example, arguments include information. These genres do not always appear in isolation and should not always be taught that way.

☐ When designing writing prompts, consider trying to make them more authentic. Authentic prompts involve topics and issues that students might face in their communities or see in the world around them. Authentic prompts will motivate students because they'll see the real-life purpose of the assignment. Also use authentic audiences, and submit students' work to those audiences; don't have students write just "for the teacher." They will be more motivated to revise and polish their writing when they know that the "outside world" will see it.

☐ Assign a mix of short and long research projects.

☐ Teach students to be aware of audience and adjust their language accordingly. They should understand when to write in a more formal or less formal style.

☐ Consider problem- and project-based learning as a realistic, 21st-century way to teach research and writing. For more on these areas, see Edutopia's Project-Based Learning site: www.edutopia.org/project-based-learning. Also see *Students Taking Charge: Inside the Learner-Active, Technology-Infused Classroom,* by Nancy Sulla (2011, Eye On Education), which contains examples of problem-based learning across the content areas as well as guidelines for designing your own assignments.

☐ Have students use technology to produce and publish writing, as required by the standards. Think of innovative ways that students can produce and publish writing on blogs and wikis and use other online tools so real audiences can read their work.

☐ The Common Core State Standards do not cover teaching students to write poetry, but they do say that you can include it (and other forms of creative writing) if you wish. See The Common Core State Standards, Appendix A, page 23.

☐ Teach argument, not persuasion. The Common Core State Standards draw a distinction between the two.

> A logical argument . . . convinces the audience because of the perceived merit and reasonableness of the claims and proofs offered rather than either the emotions the writing evokes in the audience or the character or credentials of the writer. (Common Core State Standards, p. 24)

Persuasive writing appeals to an audience's emotions. It often depends on techniques such as bandwagon, glittering generalities, name-calling, plain folks, and snob appeal. Argument, on the other hand, appeals to logic and reason, consists of a thesis/claim and supporting evidence, and is usually written in a more formal style. The Common Core says that argument has a "special place" in the standards because it is such a crucial kind of writing to learn for college and careers. Here are some strategies for teaching this genre.

Strategies for Teaching Argument

■ Teach concession-refutation. Students should be aware of and address the other side of an issue, not just their own side.

■ Show students how to avoid common logical errors.

■ Analyze mentor texts with students. They can look for examples of concession-refutation and see how the author supports his or her claims with logical, clear evidence.

■ Teach students how to marshal facts for their arguments. Students must learn how to search for information, evaluate and sort their information, and incorporate their information effectively.

Lesson Plans at a Glance

Let Me Tell You a Legend

Writing a Narrative

Grade Levels: 6–8

Time Frame: Approximately three class periods

Overview: Though the Common Core decreases the emphasis on narrative writing in grades 6 and higher, this genre is nevertheless essential to the cumulative composition skills that students are developing. This lesson teaches narrative writing, but it also asks students to focus on key narrative elements that are integral to the analysis, reflection, and research of narrative texts.

Common Core State Standards

- 6–8: Writing, Standard 3: Write narratives to develop real or imagined experiences or events using effective technique, relevant descriptive details, and well-structured event sequences.

- 6–8: Writing, Standard 4: Produce clear and coherent writing in which the development, organization, and style are appropriate to task, purpose, and audience.

- 6–8: Writing, Standard 5: With some guidance and support from peers and adults, develop and strengthen writing as needed by planning, revising, editing, rewriting, or trying a new approach.

- 6: Reading, Literature, Standard 3: Describe how a particular story's or drama's plot unfolds in a series of episodes as well as how the characters respond or change as the plot moves toward a resolution.

- 7: Reading, Literature, Standard 3: Analyze how particular elements of a story or drama interact (e.g., how setting shapes the character or plot).

- 8: Reading, Literature, Standard 3: Analyze how particular lines of dialogue or incidents in a story or drama propel the action, reveal aspects of a character, or provoke a decision.

- 6–8: Speaking and Listening, Standard 1: Engage effectively in a range of collaborative discussions . . . with diverse partners . . . building on others' ideas and expressing their own clearly.

Objectives

- Students will use a well-structured event sequence to write a narrative that develops the experience of a legendary hero.

- Students will establish a setting, pace events to create rising and falling action, and include a theme or moral.

Background Knowledge Required

Students should be familiar with terms related to studying and writing narratives, including *character*, *setting*, *event*, *sequence of events*, and *theme*.

Materials Needed

- Copies of the handout: Story Planning Sheet, p. 60

Agenda

1. **Introduction**: Write the name *Robin Hood* on the board. Tell students that, as they probably know, Robin Hood is a legendary hero. A legend is a traditional story about a famous person or event. Legends are usually based on historical fact, but over time, the truth of the events and the person stretch to legendary proportions. In some cases, as with Robin Hood, no one is sure whether the legendary hero was even a real person. On the board, beneath *Robin Hood*, draw a table with four quadrants. Ask students to draw tables on their own paper and take notes along with you. Label the quadrants "Time and Place," "Character Traits," "Events," and "Theme or Moral." Taking the quadrants one by one, ask students to tell you what they know about Robin Hood. When a few items have been listed in each quadrant (you don't need to exhaust each topic), tell students that they have the beginnings of a riveting story in their tables. In this lesson, they will write stories about their favorite legendary hero, whether it is Robin Hood or someone else. They'll use a graphic organizer such as this one to gather ideas about four key pieces of a story: setting, character, events, and theme.

2. **Full-Class Discussion**: Ask students to name other legendary heroes. If you don't have time to discuss why some of their choices are not legendary heroes (for example, they name characters from myths, fables, or fairy tales), simply write the list yourself. Examples are Joan of Arc, William Tell, King Arthur, Johnny Apple-seed, John Henry, and Calamity Jane. Have students choose one hero to write about (Robin Hood could be a choice as well), and organize students into groups based on their choices. Each group should use the table on Robin Hood as a model to create its own table, using more details, for its legendary hero.

3. **Research**: As homework, have students read a legend about the hero they chose and add useful details to the tables they created in their small groups.

4. **Planning**: At the next class meeting, draw a bell shape on the board and briefly explain the classic story structure of problem, rising action, climax, falling action, and resolution. Then have students complete the handout to plan the structures of their own stories, drawing on the work they did in their small groups. Remind them that they may not be able to use all the information from their small-group work in their work on the handout. Rather, they should pick and choose what is most useful.

5. **Drafting**: For homework, ask students to write rough drafts of their stories, drawing on the prewriting they have done. Give students specific guidelines that you choose, such as required length and format.

6. **Peer Feedback**: At the next class meeting, pass out fresh copies of the handout, and ask students to exchange story drafts with a partner. They should read their partners' stories and use details in them to fill in the handout. Afterward, the partners should return their feedback and discuss their findings, offering tips and advice as needed.

7. **Wrap-Up**: For homework, ask students to revise their stories using the feedback they received. Remind them that they do not have to use every suggestion from their partners. However, if a partner was confused about something, it is smart to revise and polish that part of the story.

Differentiation

For students who need extra support

- Plan class time for students to workshop their drafts with a second partner. Spend more time listening in and helping these students evaluate drafts.

- With the full class, review a model story written by a student. Even if the model is not a legend, you can point out strengths (vivid setting, clear sequence of events, recognizable character traits, detectable theme), pausing to ask students to how they can strengthen the same aspect of their own stories.

For advanced students

- Invite students to write longer stories in order to develop a more complex sequence of events. Encourage them to spend more time on character development, creating a fully developed villain or sidekick in addition to the fully developed hero.

Assessment

- Evaluate students' handouts. Make sure that they answered each question in each quadrant with useful information. Ask students to revise answers that are weak, irrelevant, or vague.

- Use the following rubric to evaluate students' stories.

Score 4.0	The story • Has a vivid setting, including such details as historical time period, geographic place, time of day, buildings, vegetation, etc. • Has a legendary hero with character traits that show why he or she would engage in the events and that help make the theme clear. • Has a well-structured sequence of events that includes a problem, increasing tension, a high point of action, decreasing tension, and closure. • Has a theme or moral that grows out of the hero's actions and the events. No major errors or omissions in the score 4.0 content.
Score 3.5	The student demonstrates success at the 3.0 level plus partial success at the 4.0 level.

Score 3.0	The story • Has an identifiable setting. • Has a legendary hero with one or two specific character traits. • Has a sequence of events that includes a problem, efforts to solve the problem, and closure. • Has a theme or moral, though it may be hard to identify. No major errors or omissions in the score 3.0 content.
Score 2.5	The student demonstrates success at the 2.0 level plus partial success at the 3.0 level.
Score 2.0	The story • Has a vague or simplistic setting. • Has a legendary hero, though her or his character traits are not clear. • Has a series of events that begins with a problem, though the events are confusing, seem out of order, or don't clearly relate to one another. No major errors or omissions in the score 2.0 content.
Score 1.5	The student demonstrates partial success at the 2.0 level; the setting or the main problem may be omitted.
Score 1.0	With help, the student achieves partial success at score 2.0 and 3.0 contents.
Score 0.5	With help, the student achieves partial success at score 2.0 content but not score 3.0 content.
Score 0.0	Even with help, the student has no success.

Additional Resources

- You can find stories written by teenagers to use as models at Teen Ink: www.teenink .com.

Notes

After implementing the lesson, reflect on what worked and what you would change next time.

_____

_____

_____

_____

Story Planning Sheet

Use the following chart to help plan the story you are writing. Use extra paper or write on the back if you need more space.

Time and Place (Setting)	Characters
1. Around what time in history does your legend take place?	**1.** Who is your legendary hero?
2. Where in the world does it take place?	**2.** What adjectives could you use to describe this character? Be specific. Instead of *heroic*, use words such as *brave* or *selfless*.
3. What are the surroundings like during much of the story? For example, does it take place in a forest, on a prairie, on a battlefield, etc.? Name the type of place and provide descriptive details.	**3.** Who is working against the hero? This is usually a villain or an enemy.
	4. What adjectives could you use to describe this character?

Events	Theme
1. What problem must your hero solve?	**1.** What noun could you use to express the theme of your story? *Justice* might be an example.
2. What event gets the story started?	**2.** How could you express the theme in a complete sentence? Ask yourself, "What does the story say about the noun I wrote in step 1?"
3. What does your hero do next? ▪ ▪ ▪ ▪	**3.** Which actions or character traits best support the theme of your story? ▪ ▪ ▪ ▪
4. How does the hero solve the problem? This will be the climax, or highest point of action.	
5. What happens next? How does the story end?	

I've Got Questions. Who Has Answers?

Conduct a Research Project

Grade Levels: 6–8

Time Frame: Approximately two or three class periods

Overview: This lesson takes students through a step-by-step research process. It uses the topic of family vacations, but you can adapt the lesson to use a topic that students are researching in your class or another class. To increase the complexity of the lesson for advanced students or students in grade 8, spend more time teaching and practicing the art of generating focused questions and using multiple types of media to gather information. Note that this lesson focuses on research for informative or explanatory texts, but the research skills that students learn will also come into play when they do argument writing because it's necessary to do research to gather facts for that genre as well.

This lesson discusses a natural disaster; you may wish to involve a science teacher in your planning.

Common Core State Standards

- 6–8: Writing, Standard 2: Write informative/explanatory texts to examine a topic and convey ideas, concepts, and information through the selection, organization, and analysis of relevant content.

- 6–8: Writing, Standard 4: Produce clear and coherent writing in which the development, organization, and style are appropriate to task, purpose, and audience.

- 6: Writing, Standard 7: Conduct short research projects to answer a question, drawing on several sources and refocusing the inquiry when appropriate.

- 7: Writing, Standard 7: Conduct short research projects to answer a question, drawing on several sources and generating additional related, focused questions for further research and investigation.

- 8: Writing, Standard 7: Conduct short research projects to answer a question (including a self-generated question), drawing on several sources and generating additional related, focused questions that allow for multiple avenues of exploration.

- 6–8: Speaking and Listening, Standard 1: Engage effectively in a range of collaborative discussions . . . with diverse partners . . . building on others' ideas and expressing their own clearly.

Objectives

- Students will write a focused research question.

- Students will research multiple sources to answer the research question, refocusing the question as necessary.

- Students will use their research to complete a shared writing task to produce the text for an informational web page.

Background Knowledge Required

No particular background knowledge is required for this lesson.

Materials Needed

- Copies of the handout: Research Activity Sheet, p. 67

Agenda

1. **Introduction**: Begin by reading aloud a poem about Hurricane Katrina or another natural disaster. (See Additional Resources for a source of poems.) Spend a few minutes getting students' reactions to the poem. Tell students that a hurricane is one type of natural disaster. Next, tell students that the Travel Channel website has hired them to write a web page on family vacation destinations that are the sites of recent or historical natural disasters. Students will work as a full class and in small groups to research and write the informative web page.

2. **Full-Class Brainstorming Activity**: Tell students that research is all about asking and answering questions. Ask students to help you brainstorm a list of questions they could answer about family vacations on the sites of natural disasters. Examples may include the following: What is a natural disaster? What are some famous natural disasters? Is it safe to go to the site of a recent or historical natural disaster? Why would a family want to visit the site of a natural disaster?

3. **Full-Class Focusing Activity**: Explain that with any topic, the possibilities for research are practically endless. Therefore, a good research project must be focused. That means narrowing the field of research to a manageable size. Tell students to ask, "What is my purpose for writing?" and "Who is my audience?" and "What guidelines has my teacher (or boss or editor, etc.) given me?" Next, give students instructions for a writing assignment that you have created (e.g., write a web page of eight to ten paragraphs on the subject of family vacations at the sites of recent or historical natural disasters). Include your standard guidelines for written work (format, font, margins, etc.) and a deadline. Guide the students through an analysis of the written assignment by asking them to answer the questions above about writing purpose, audience, and guidelines. Then ask students to look at the list of brainstormed questions (from step 2) and decide which questions their web page will answer. Guide them to choose a number of questions based on how long the web page is supposed to be. For example, the sample questions in step 2 would be sufficient, with the bulk of the article written to expand on the question about example sites.

4. **Small-Group Research**: Organize students into small groups, and assign one research question per group. For a question about naming some famous natural

disasters, you can ask several different groups to research one example each. Have each group complete part 1 of the handout. Remind students of the context of their research: to create a web page about family vacations. Therefore, they shouldn't write a research question about a dangerous or inaccessible site of a natural disaster. At the end of the work period, each group should submit its research goal, phrased as a question. (Example: "Why would a volcano in Hawaii make a good vacation destination?")

5. **Homework**: Have students work independently to complete part 2 of the handout.

6. **Small-Group Activity**: In class the next day, have students meet with their research groups. Remind them that, just as they had to focus their research topics to make them manageable, now they need to focus their research findings to make the material manageable.

   - Students should review their research findings and decide which facts and details are most useful for creating strong answers to their research questions.
   - They should use their focused findings to create outlines for their parts of the web page. Most likely, each group will be writing one paragraph of the whole. In this case, students need to identify which part of the whole they are writing. An introduction, for example, has different requirements than a body paragraph has.
   - Each group should submit a copy of its outline to you.

7. **Homework**: Each group should write its section of the web page, following the guidelines for length and format that you specify. In addition, each group should supply a works cited page. If time allows, you may choose to have students complete the work in class, the better to facilitate gathering in groups.

8. **Wrap-Up**: Assemble the pieces of the web page in order and read them aloud to the class. Ask a few text-based questions, such as "Why is (name a natural disaster site in the web page) a good choice for a family vacation?" or "Why would (identify a particular paragraph) appeal to the target audience?" or "How does the introductory paragraph capture readers' attention?" Read individual paragraphs aloud again if necessary. Then ask volunteers to share helpful tips for researching an informational topic. They may offer suggestions about using focused search terms in a web browser, asking a librarian for help, eliminating unreliable sources, etc.

Extend the Lesson

- Use this lesson in conjunction with Lesson Plan 14 on page 69.

- Teach the proper format for creating a works cited page.

Differentiation

For students who need extra support

- Give students paragraph maps to use as examples in the small-group activity. Types of paragraphs should include introduction, body paragraph, and conclusion. For example, a body paragraph might begin with a topic sentence followed by several sentences that support, explain, or illustrate the topic; a conclusion sentence ties together the ideas in the paragraph.

- Allow students to work with their groups or partners from their groups to complete part 2 of the handout.

For advanced students

- When assigning students to groups, consider grouping advanced students in pairs or threes so that each student carries a greater responsibility for completing the work.

- Schedule a brief discussion time to follow each small-group activity. Ask volunteers to give examples of how they completed a task. Use their responses as an opportunity to troubleshoot problems that struggling students may be having.

Assessment

- Check each group's research question to make sure it is focused and relevant to the assignment. Ask the group to narrow the focus (perhaps by using a proper noun instead of a general term) if necessary.

- While small groups evaluate their research findings, monitor their discussions. Watch for examples of reliable, solid, or well-targeted research and share that example with the class. (Example: "This group found facts about a tsunami on the National Oceanic and Atmospheric Administration website, which is a government website. This is an example of a reliable source.")

- Review each group's outline. Check for the proper format of introduction, body paragraph, and conclusion. If necessary, have students revise their outlines in response to your feedback (e.g., arrange information in a logical order; eliminate weak, vague, or redundant points; cut the outline down to size per the length requirement).

- Assess each group's paragraph/section and works cited list using the following rubric.

Score 4.0	The group • Writes a focused, informative piece of the web page. • Uses relevant ideas, facts, details, and/or examples. • Selects information appropriate for an audience of families planning a vacation. • Arranges the paragraph's topic sentence and information logically. • Cites reliable sources of information. No major errors or omissions in the score 4.0 content.
Score 3.5	The group demonstrates success at the 3.0 level plus partial success at the 4.0 level.
Score 3.0	The group • Writes an informative piece of the web page, but it lacks a tight focus. • Uses ideas, facts, details, and/or examples, but one or two are vague, irrelevant, or redundant. • Arranges sentences logically, with one or two exceptions. • Cites sources of information but includes an unreliable source. No major errors or omissions in the score 3.0 content.

Score 2.5	The group demonstrates success at the 2.0 level plus partial success at the 3.0 level.
Score 2.0	The group • Writes a piece of the web page that does not clearly connect to the class's outline OR uses a predominantly persuasive or narrative approach. • Offers too few supporting details OR details that are vague, irrelevant, or redundant. • Arranges sentences in a mostly random manner. • Cites no sources of information. No major errors or omissions in the score 2.0 content.
Score 1.5	The group demonstrates partial success at the 2.0 level.
Score 1.0	With help, the group achieves partial success at score 2.0 and 3.0 contents.
Score 0.5	With help, the group achieves partial success at score 2.0 content but not score 3.0 content.
Score 0.0	Even with help, the group has no success.

Additional Resources

- You can find poems about Hurricane Katrina at the Katrina Poems website: www.msstate.edu/dept/IH/KatrinaSubmissions.html.

- A step-by-step guide for performing research at the middle-school level is available on the Alexandria Country Day School website: www.acdsnet.org/uploads/file/library/MS_Research_Guide.pdf. It includes useful sections on plagiarism and outline format.

- The Purdue Online Writing Lab has helpful pages on these topics:

  - Conducting research: owl.english.purdue.edu/owl/section/2/8
  - Using MLA format to create a works cited page: owl.english.purdue.edu/owl/section/2/11

Notes

After implementing the lesson, reflect on what worked and what you would change next time.

_____

_____

_____

_____

Name: _____   Date: _____

Research Activity Sheet

Part 1: Plan your research by completing each item below.

---

1. Write your research question.
Example: Which volcano in the United States would be a good place for a family vacation?

Your research question: _____

_____

---

2. List search terms (words and phrases) that will help you find information to answer your research question.
Examples: *volcano United States, volcano vacation, volcanoes to visit, family volcano vacation*

Your search terms:

-
-
-
-
-

3. Once you perform a few searches, focus your search terms. For example, *volcanoes in Hawaii* is more focused than *volcano United States. Hawai'i Volcanoes National Park* is more focused than *volcanoes in Hawaii.*

Your focused search terms:

-
-
-
-
-

Part 2: Carry out your research by completing each item below.

1. Perform a search for information in at least TWO different formats. For example, search for websites and search for books. List three to five reliable sources below, and write a brief note about how each source can help you answer your research question.	

Source	How It Is Helpful
Example: *Source and publication information:* Hawai'i Volcanoes National Park, www.nps.gov/havo/index.htm	Example: Tells how to plan a short or long vacation to see the volcanoes. Has sections titled Nature & Science and History & Culture.
Source 1	
Source 2	
Source 3	
Source 4	
Source 5	

2. Check off each task below as you complete it.

- Review the research question in part 1, item 1.
- Review the sources you found in part 2, above, and put stars by the TWO sources that would best help you answer the research question.
- Gather useful facts and ideas from each starred source by taking notes, marking up printouts or photocopies, or attaching and writing on sticky notes.
- Take this work with you to class to help complete the next part of your research assignment.

What's Google Giving You?

Evaluating Your Sources

14

Grade Levels: 6–8

Time Frame: Approximately one or two class periods

Overview: This lesson teaches students how to gather and incorporate evidence from reliable sources. Students are often tempted to just Google a topic and trust the first site they see; this lesson shows them how to carefully consider a source before using it. This lesson plan involves gathering facts for an informational essay, but it can easily be modified to teach marshaling facts for an argument.

Common Core State Standards
- 6: Writing, Standard 8: Gather relevant information from multiple print and digital sources; assess the credibility of each source.
- 7–8: Writing, Standard 8: Gather relevant information from multiple print and digital sources; . . . assess the credibility and accuracy of each source.

Objectives
- Students will look at the URL of a site (.com, .gov, .org, blogspot.com, en.wikipedia .org, etc.) and identify what kind of site it might be (official government site, a site to which anyone can contribute, etc.).

- Students will examine which kinds of sites would be the most useful for different purposes and information needs.

- Students will evaluate a source's accuracy, currency, and reliability.

Background Knowledge Required
Students should be beginning an informational essay on a topic that you assign or that students select.

Materials Needed
- Copies of the handout: Analyzing a Website Activity Sheet, p. 72

Agenda
1. **Introduction**: Ask students if they've ever looked up a health or nutrition topic online. Let's say a student sprains an ankle playing soccer and wants to know how to treat it. How can the student know the info is reliable? Is info from a chat room the same as info from a doctor? How can a person tell? Is information from a company

that's selling ankle support guards as reliable as information from a health organization? Make a list of students' responses on the board. From their responses (and your own additions), decide as a class on the criteria that should be used when evaluating a website. Criteria should include currency (When was the site last updated?), author/agency (Is there bias? Is someone trying to sell something?), and reliability (Is there a list of sources? Were experts consulted?). Point out to students that the ending of a URL can offer a clue about the website's accuracy, which means searchers can narrow results before analyzing sites. For example, .gov means it's a government website, and .org could mean that it's a nonprofit organization.

2. **Activity**: Do part 1 of the handout as a full class. Then have students do part 2 independently. Go over their answers as a class.

3. **Wrap-Up**: Assign part 3 of the handout for homework.

Extend the Lesson

- Display sample websites on a whiteboard, and have students point out where the "last updated" and "about the author" info appears. Ask students where a researcher can find out if the author of the site is an expert or consulted expert sources. Ask students if there is evidence of bias.

- Look at the sites as a class. Have students analyze sites on all kinds of informational topics throughout the year; they need to develop this skill for high school and beyond.

Differentiation

For students who need extra support
- Provide more examples of each type of website (.gov, .com, etc.). Give students a list of topics from which to choose for part 3 of the handout.

For advanced students
- Have students do Internet research on a more complex topic and evaluate each source.

Assessment

- Evaluate the three parts of the handout to make sure that students understand how to sort through search results and evaluate a site.

- Require the use of accurate sources for writing and research projects throughout the year.

Additional Resources

- The following site offers questions to ask when evaluating a website: www.lib .berkeley.edu/TeachingLib/Guides/Internet/Evaluate.html.

Notes

After implementing the lesson, reflect on what worked and what you would change the next time.

_____

_____

_____

_____

Analyzing a Website Activity Sheet

Part 1: Fill in the table that follows.

URL component	What it means	Why might you use this kind of site?
.com		
.gov		
.org		
blogspot.com		
en.wikipedia.org		

Part 2: Below is part of a search-results page. Use these search results to answer the questions that follow.

Sprained ankle - Wikipedia, the free encyclopedia
en.wikipedia.org/wiki/Sprained_ankle
A sprained ankle, also known as an ankle sprain, twisted ankle, rolled ankle, ankle injury or ankle ligament injury, is a common medical condition where one or . . .

Ankle Sprain Causes, Symptoms, Treatments, Recovery
www.webmd.com/a-to-z-guides/ankle-sprain-overview
May 19, 2011 - What is an ankle sprain? Most people have twisted an ankle at some point in their life. But if your ankle gets swollen and painful after you twist it, . . .

Sprained Ankle - OrthoInfo - AAOS
orthoinfo.aaos.org/topic.cfm?topic=a00150
A sprained ankle is a very common injury. Approximately 25,000 people experience it each day. A sprained ankle can happen to athletes and non-athletes, . . .

A Fast **Sprained Ankle** Treatment - Heal in Days, Not Weeks
www.asprainedankle.com/
Dec 20, 2011 - We guarantee you will be PAIN FREE in 3-7 days by using the proven H.E.M. Sprained Ankle Rehab System. Don't rely on R.I.C.E. (rest, ice, . . .

Ankle pain: MedlinePlus Medical Encyclopedia
www.nlm.nih.gov/medlineplus/ency/article/003167.htm
In addition to ankle sprains, ankle pain can be caused by: . . . stress off your ankle for up to 10 days for a milder sprain and 2 to 5 weeks for a more severe sprain.

1. Which site(s) would you visit if you were writing a paper about treating common sports injuries, including ankle sprains? Explain.

2. Which site is selling something? Would this site be a reliable source of information? Why or why not?

3. Which site contains information that anyone can add to or change? What are the benefits and drawbacks of using that kind of site to find facts?

Part 3: Go online and check out the websites listed in part 2. Look at them closely. Then complete the table. Use separate paper if necessary.

Criteria	Website 1	Website 2	Website 3	Website 4	Website 5
URL					
Author/agency behind the site					
Who wrote or reviewed the medical information?					
When was the site last updated?					
Comprehensiveness of information					
Clarity of information					

Which websites seemed to be the most trustworthy? Explain.

74

To Quote or Not to Quote?

Incorporating Your Sources

Grade Levels: 6–8

Time Frame: Approximately one or two class periods

Overview: This lesson will help students understand when to paraphrase, when to quote, and how to avoid plagiarism. It will also show students how to incorporate quotations into a text.

Common Core State Standards
- 6–8: Writing, Standard 8: Gather relevant information from multiple print and digital sources; . . . quote or paraphrase the data and conclusions of others while avoiding plagiarism.

Objectives
- Students will learn to make decisions about paraphrasing or quoting.
- Students will understand what constitutes plagiarism and learn what paraphrasing really means.
- Students will practice incorporating quotations into their writing.

Background Knowledge Required
Students should have experience conducting research and recording where they find their information.

Materials Needed
- Copies of the handout: Ways to Incorporate Sources, p. 78

Agenda
1. **Introduction**: Tell students that they've spent time learning how to evaluate sources and find information, and now they're going to discuss how to incorporate that information into an essay.

2. **Mini-Lesson**: Write *paraphrase vs. quote* on the board. Ask students to consider when they might want to paraphrase information and when they might need to quote it. Why would it matter to readers? Mention that general, common-sense information does not need to be quoted.

3. **Independent Work**: Give students the handout on how to paraphrase and how to incorporate quotes. Go over it as a class, and have students complete the practice exercises on their own.

4. **Full-Class Discussion**: Go over the practice exercises as a full class. When you go over paraphrasing, discuss that changing only a word or two constitutes plagiarism. Students should alter sentence structure, consider which words are replaceable, combine sentences, and decide what to leave out and what to keep from the original. Also discuss the importance of citing sources.

Extend the Lesson

- Do a follow-up lesson on using MLA style to cite sources in the text and reference them in a bibliography.

Differentiation

For students who need extra support

- Give them easier passages to paraphrase, and help them practice summarizing information from a source.

For advanced students

- Have them work with information from more complex sources.

Assessment

- Evaluate students' handouts to see whether they effectively paraphrased and explained quotations.

- Make sure that students continue to practice these skills throughout the year. When you assess students' writing, include incorporating sources on the rubrics you use.

Additional Resources

- This page provides additional practice on quoting, paraphrasing, and summarizing: owl.english.purdue.edu/owl/resource/563/01.

- The University of Houston at Victoria has a helpful guide to deciding when to quote, paraphrase, or summarize: www.uhv.edu/ac/style/pdf/quote.pdf.

- This page provides examples of successful and unsuccessful paraphrases: writing.wisc .edu/Handbook/QPA_paraphrase.html.

- Purdue Online provides a quick guide to citing sources using MLA style: owl.english .purdue.edu/owl/resource/747/01.

Notes

After implementing the lesson, reflect on what worked and what you would change the next time.

_____

_____

_____

_____

Ways to Incorporate Sources

Imagine that you are writing an informational essay on how chocolate bars are made. Below is one of the sources you found. What would you paraphrase, summarize, and quote? Read the paragraph and complete the exercises that follow.

How Chocolate Is Made
Laura Martin

The process of making a chocolate bar takes a long time and involves many steps. Chocolate comes from *Theobroma cacao* trees, which thrive in tropical locations near the equator. (So unfortunately, you can't grow one in your own backyard!) These trees produce large, oblong cacao pods, which can be as large as a football. When the pods are ripe, they are harvested and then opened to remove the cocoa beans. The cocoa beans are actually bitter, not sweet. The bitterness is removed by fermenting the beans and then drying them outside in large baskets. Once that process is complete, the beans are sent to factories around the world, such as Hershey's, Nestlé, Ghirardelli, and Scharffen Berger. The factories roast the cocoa beans to bring out the flavor, and then winnow the beans. Winnowing means removing the bean shells and revealing the cocoa nibs inside. The nibs are ground into a paste and mixed with other ingredients, such as sugar and milk, depending on a company's chocolate bar recipe. Milk chocolate requires more add-ins than dark chocolate. Next, the paste is conched, which smooths out the paste, and tempered, which cools it. Finally, the bars are shaped, wrapped, and sent to your local supermarket. It's a long process, but it's worth it—chocolate not only tastes great but also has certain health benefits and is known to improve people's moods. In this country, chocolate is popular not just on Valentine's Day but year round. In fact, the average person in the U.S. eats about 12 pounds of chocolate every year!

Paraphrasing shows your understanding of the content. Make sure to paraphrase fully by changing the wording and sentence structures. Don't replace just one or two words here or there. If you don't know what a word means, don't blindly include it in your paraphrase. For example, if you don't know what *fermenting* is, look it up and put it in your own words rather than putting it in a paraphrase that has no meaning to you.

Example: The beans are shelled through the process of winnowing. Underneath the shells are the cocoa nibs.

Now you try it. Pick a sentence from the article, and paraphrase it below:

_____

_____

_____

_____

_____

Summarizing also shows your understanding of the content.

Example: Making chocolate requires numerous steps, from harvesting the cacao pods to making a paste to shaping and smoothing out the chocolate.

Now you try it. In the space below, summarize something from the article:

_____

_____

_____

_____

_____

Quoting is useful when you want to be able to use the author's expertise. It is also good to quote when the author's wording is clever or catchy and paraphrasing it wouldn't have the same impact. Be careful not to quote too often, though. It can bog down your essay. You should also be careful not to throw the quotes into your essay; make sure you provide context and explain them.

Example: According to Laura Martin, "the average person in the U.S. eats about 12 pounds of chocolate every year."

Now you try it. Pick something to quote from the article, and write it below.

_____

_____

_____

_____

_____

Collaborate in the Cloud

Creating a Literature Guide Wiki

Grade Levels: 6–8

Time Frame: Approximately one class period

Overview: In this lesson, students will create wiki guides to a novel they are reading in class.

Common Core State Standards

- 6: Writing, Standard 6: Use technology, including the Internet, to produce and publish writing as well as to interact and collaborate with others.

- 7: Writing, Standard 6: Use technology, including the Internet, to produce and publish writing and link to and cite sources as well as to interact and collaborate with others, including linking to and citing sources.

- 8: Writing, Standard 6: Use technology, including the Internet, to produce and publish writing and present the relationships between information and ideas efficiently as well as to interact and collaborate with others.

- 6: Writing, Standard 9: Draw evidence from literary or informational texts to support analysis, reflection, and research. a. Apply *grade 6 Reading standards* to literature.

- 7: Writing, Standard 9: Draw evidence from literary or informational texts to support analysis, reflection, and research. a. Apply *grade 7 Reading standards* to literature.

- 8: Writing, Standard 9: Draw evidence from literary or informational texts to support analysis, reflection, and research. a. Apply *grade 8 Reading standards* to literature.

Objectives

- Students will think critically about a literary text.

- Students will use technology to share their ideas on the text with one another.

Background Knowledge Required

Students should be reading a literary text in class. They should begin the wiki while they are still reading the text and complete the wiki when they are done with the text.

Before giving this lesson, you should set up a class wiki on the text students are reading. Choose a school-friendly wiki site, such as PBworks, Wetpaint, or Wikispaces. Add categories to the wiki: characters, setting, themes. You can also add other categories, such as a summary or an analysis of each chapter or famous quotes with an analysis of each.

Materials Needed
- Computers with access to the wiki you have set up.
- Copies of the literary text that students are reading in class.

Agenda
1. **Introduction**: Tell students that they are going to write a wiki literary guide to the text, in which they analyze and write about the major characters, setting, and themes. They will write the guide collaboratively, sharing ideas about what they've read. Ask students: What are the benefits to this kind of collaborative writing? (Helps writers consider multiple perspectives, allows the inclusion of helpful links, helps writers study and review material with other people, etc.) What might be tricky about this kind of collaborative writing? (Writers can edit one another's work, etc.) Have students jot down some ideas on a piece of paper.

2. **Partner Activity**: Have students work in pairs. Assign each pair a character, the setting, or a major theme. Each pair should brainstorm what they'd like to include for their section. Make sure that students refer to the text during this exercise. Later or the next day, have students work on the computers and log into the class wiki. Each pair should create a section on its assigned topic. Then give pairs the opportunity to review, add to, and edit the other sections of the wiki. Go over class rules for editing one another's sections respectfully.

3. **Wrap-Up**: Have students reflect on their experience creating the wiki. They should refer to the notes they jotted at the beginning of the lesson to see how their ideas changed.

Extend the Lesson
- Require that students use graphics and other visuals to enhance their wiki entries. Discuss the importance of visuals to teach and not just to decorate.

Differentiation
For students who need extra support
- Provide more brainstorming time so students can flesh out their answers. Pair more tech-savvy students with less tech-savvy ones so they can help one another.

For advanced students
- Have students contribute content to additional sections of the wiki and/or do their literary guides for a different text they have read.

Assessment
- Evaluate students' contributions to their own sections of the wiki as well as their edits or additions to the other sections.
- You may want to create a rubric for evaluating wikis (with students' assistance) and make sure students are familiar with it before they begin writing. Categories could

include thoroughness of content, clarity of the organizational structure, accessibility of the language, and correct use of mechanics.

Additional Resources

- This page suggests fun ways to use wikis in the classroom: www.smartteaching .org/blog/2008/08/50-ways-to-use-wikis-for-a-more-collaborative-and-interactive -classroom.

- The Cool Cat Teacher Blog provides tips and ideas for using wikis in your lessons: coolcatteacher.blogspot.com/2005/12/wiki-wiki-teaching-art-of-using-wiki.html.

Notes

After implementing the lesson, reflect on what worked and what you would change the next time.

_____

_____

_____

_____

Clean-Up Time

Edit the Wordiness from Your Writing

Grade Level: 7 (but can also be done in grade 6)

Time Frame: Approximately one class period

Overview: This lesson shows students how to reduce wordiness in their writing. Do this lesson once students have an essay in its final stages.

Common Core State Standards

- 7: Language, Standard 3: Use knowledge of language and its conventions when writing, speaking, reading, or listening. a. Choose language that expresses ideas precisely and concisely, recognizing and eliminating wordiness and redundancy.

- 6–7: Writing, Standard 6: Use technology, including the Internet, to produce and publish writing.

- 6–7: Writing, Standard 5: With some guidance and support from peers and adults, develop and strengthen writing as needed by planning, revising, editing, rewriting, or trying a new approach.

Objectives

- Students will think critically about making word choices and omitting unnecessary words.

- Students will revise their writing for needless words and phrases.

Background Knowledge Required

Students should know how to write different types of sentences.

Materials Needed

- Students' essays

Agenda

1. **Introduction:** Tell students that their essays are going to be published in an electronic newsletter, but they need to cut their essays to fit the layouts and allow for photos and other visuals. How do they decide what words to cut? Tell them that they might have a lot of "weeds" (unnecessary words) in their essays; cutting them will improve the layout and, more important, make their essays cleaner and easier to follow.

2. **Mini-Lesson**: On a whiteboard or an overhead, put up three different sentences.

   - In my personal opinion, chocolate tastes better than vanilla.
   - Because of the fact that he didn't do his homework, he didn't understand the lesson.
   - The pasta had a really nice smell.

   Ask students to look for the "weeds" in each one. Have students come up with ways to cut each sentence. Then point out that each sentence demonstrates a different thing to look for when reducing wordiness.

   - The first sentence demonstrates redundancies. *My personal opinion* could be *my opinion*; the *my* already says it's personal.
   - The second sentence is an example of meaningless expressions. *Because of the fact that he didn't do his homework* could be shortened to *Because he didn't do his homework.*
   - The third sentence is an example of vague words that could be replaced with one, more precise word. *Fragrant* could replace *really nice smell.* (The pasta was *fragrant.*)

   You can also tie in the parts of speech to this lesson. Teach students that if they let verbs and nouns do the heavy lifting, their sentences will be more concise. They can delete superfluous prepositional phrases, and they can also eliminate some adverbs and adjectives by choosing specific nouns and verbs.

3. **Independent Activity**: Have students apply this lesson to their own essays. They should revise their essays and consider which words don't carry their weight.

Extend the Lesson

- Follow up on this lesson throughout the year as students complete different types of writing assignments in class.

- Have students read the chapter on clutter from William Zinsser's *On Writing Well* and the section on omitting needless words from Strunk and White's *The Elements of Style.*

Differentiation

For students who need extra support

- Spend more time on each type of wordiness. Have students do peer editing with partners who can help them find words to cut.

For advanced students

- Have students edit their essays for more complex types of wordiness, such as unnecessary adjectives that could be eliminated by choosing more precise nouns.

Assessment

- Check students' work during the cutting activity to make sure they understood the mini-lesson.

- Evaluate students' final essays for wordiness. You can include wordiness as a criterion on the rubric you use to assess their essays.

Additional Resources

- This web page contains a helpful list of things to look for when reducing wordiness: www.wm.edu/as/history/undergraduateprogram/historywritingresourcecenter/handouts/reducingwordiness/index.php.

Notes

After implementing the lesson, reflect on what worked and what you would change the next time.

_____

_____

_____

_____

Do They Know What You Know?

Describing Technical Information to an Audience

Lesson Plan 18

Grade Levels: 6–8

Time Frame: Approximately one class period

Overview: In this lesson, students will learn to consider their audience when making writing decisions. Students will practice adjusting their language and word choices to suit different audiences and purposes.

This lesson uses earthquakes as the topic. You might wish to involve science teachers in your planning.

Common Core State Standards

- 6–8: Writing, Standard 2: Write informative/explanatory texts to examine a topic and convey ideas, concepts, and information through the selection, organization, and analysis of relevant content. d. Use precise language and domain-specific vocabulary to inform about or explain the topic.

- 6–8: Writing, Standard 10: Write routinely over extended time frames . . . and shorter time frames . . . for a range of discipline-specific tasks, purposes, and audiences.

Objectives

- Students will adjust their word choices, sentence structures, and tone for different audiences.

- Students will write in different styles for audiences with different levels of background knowledge on a topic.

Background Knowledge Required

This lesson should be done toward the beginning of an informational writing unit. Students should not have done any drafting at this point.

Materials Needed

- Students' notes for their informational essays

Agenda

1. **Introduction**: Tell students that today, the class will discuss audience. How might students' informational writing change based on their audience? Have them spend a few minutes jotting down some possible responses.

2. **Mini-Lesson**: Ask students to imagine that they are experts on earthquakes (or some other topic of your choosing). How would they present that information differently to

   - elementary-school kids?
   - other experts on earthquakes?
   - residents of a town hit by earthquakes?
   - residents of an area where earthquakes rarely hit?

   Write all four possible audiences on the board. Discuss as a class how the tone and the amount of background knowledge a writer provides would vary depending on the audience's experience with the topic. For example, elementary-school kids would need a basic definition of earthquakes with examples and visuals. Other earthquake experts would not need such a definition of earthquake; that could seem condescending. The writing could include sophisticated language and terms used without definitions. You may wish to discuss the differences among Tier One (everyday speech), Two (general academic words), and Three (domain-specific words) with students.

   Residents in an earthquake-prone area would be familiar with earthquake safety, but they are not scientists, so writing would need to be very clear and include explanations of terms used. A writer would have to be even clearer when writing for residents in areas that never experience earthquakes; they have even less familiarity with the topic. Tell students that level of experience is not the only factor to consider. They also have to consider context. Is the audience hearing this info on *Good Morning America* or reading about it in the *New York Times*, in a scientific journal, or on a student's blog? Are audience members young or old?

3. **Independent Work**: Assign students two different audiences for the informational essays they are working on in class. Have them write a sample paragraph for each audience, considering the elements you discussed as a class.

4. **Wrap-Up**: Have students discuss and/or write reflections on what they did differently for each version. Then assign the audience that students will ultimately use when they draft their full essays, or allow them to choose the one that they prefer and write their full essays for that audience.

Extend the Lesson

- Ask students to gather a bunch of articles on the same topic from different kinds of publications for different audiences. Give them guidelines about where to find such articles. Students should write brief analyses of how each source presents information for that publication's audience. They should use specific examples from each source.

- When students complete their drafts, have them work with partners to review one another's work and make sure that the language and tone for the chosen audience are consistent throughout the essays.

Differentiation

For students who need extra support

- Spend more time helping students with word choice and language decisions for various audiences.

For advanced students

- Require that students use even more domain-specific (Tier Three) words in their essays.

Assessment

- Evaluate whether students' essays demonstrate an awareness of audience, as evidenced by their language, word choices, and tone. Make sure to include audience awareness on the rubric you use to assess their essays.

- Check students' reflections for understanding of how writing changes based on audience.

Additional Resources

- This page from Colorado State University provides a helpful list of questions to consider when analyzing audience: writing.colostate.edu/guides/processes/audmod/com2c2.cfm.

Notes

After implementing the lesson, reflect on what worked and what you would change the next time.

Hook People In!

Introducing Your Information

Grade Levels: 7–8; can be adapted down to grade 6 (see note in Overview)

Time Frame: Approximately one class period

Overview: This lesson shows students how to write clear introductions that lay out what they will discuss in their essays. Do this lesson when you are teaching informational writing, after students have gathered their facts and are ready to begin writing.

To adapt this lesson down to grade 6, teach students how to introduce a topic clearly; you don't need to cover how an introduction should preview what's to follow.

Common Core State Standards

- 7–8: Writing, Standard 2: Write informative/explanatory texts to examine a topic and convey ideas, concepts, and information through the selection, organization, and analysis of relevant content. a. Introduce a concept clearly, previewing what is to follow; organize ideas, concepts, and information.

- 7–8: Writing, Standard 10: Write routinely over extended time frames . . . and shorter time frames . . . for a range of discipline-specific tasks, purposes, and audiences.

Objectives

- Students will consider how to clearly introduce a topic to an audience.

- Students will practice writing introductory paragraphs to informational essays.

Background Knowledge Required

Students should have experience gathering facts for informational essays and should have some knowledge of writing thesis statements.

Materials Needed

- Students should come to class prepared with the notes/information they have gathered for their essays. They should have decided on the organizational plan and audience for their essays.

Agenda

1. **Introduction**: Write *thesis* on the board, and ask students what it means; they should have some prior experience with a thesis statement from previous years. Write some sample thesis statements on the board (on a topic related to what you assigned for the informational essay), and have students decide whether they are solid.

2. **Full-Class Discussion**: Ask students what else an introductory paragraph should include. It should outline the main points they plan to make (preview what's to follow) and also reflect the organizational pattern they will use. Show examples of strong introductions (on related topics) on the board, and ask students to point out why they are strong. It would be helpful to show real-world examples from a variety of publications. You can also discuss the importance of making the introduction engaging. Students can begin with an intriguing story (anecdote), begin by asking a question, or begin by stating an alarming statistic. They should avoid the "In this essay, I'm going to tell you about" form or the dictionary definition form. Have students recall what they learned about audience from Lesson 18 and how audience might affect how they introduce their topics.

3. **Independent Work**: Have students write introductory paragraphs to their informational essays.

4. **Partner Work**: Have partners read each other's intros and describe exactly what the essays will be about. If they are wrong, perhaps the writer needs to tweak something to make the intro clearer to others.

5. **Wrap-Up**: Students should revise their essays based on the partner activity.

Extend the Lesson

- Have students complete their drafts. Later, you may wish to do a mini-lesson on conclusion writing.

Differentiation

For students who need extra support
- Provide more examples of effective and ineffective introductions.

- Spend more time on crafting a thesis.

- Work one-on-one with some students to ensure that their thesis statements are clear and focused. Provide sentence frames to help students write theses and introductory paragraphs.

For advanced students
- Have the more sophisticated writers help others with their introductions.

Assessment

- Evaluate students' participation during the class activity in which they analyzed model introductions.

- Assess students' introductory paragraphs based on what you taught during this lesson.

Additional Resources

- This web page lists common pitfalls when writing an introduction, such as apologizing or announcing intentions: grammar.ccc.commnet.edu/grammar/intros.htm.

Notes

After implementing the lesson, reflect on what worked and what you would change the next time.

_____

_____

_____

_____

I Say Tomato, You Say To-Mah-To

Effective Argument Techniques

Grade Levels: 7–8; can be adapted to grade 6 (see note under Overview)

Time Frame: Approximately one class period

Overview: This lesson should be done during a unit on argument writing. It will help students identify and organize strong reasons and evidence to use in writing arguments. This lesson also teaches students to identify and respond to an opposing claim (concession-refutation). You can adapt the lesson to grade 6 by omitting references to opposing claims.

Common Core State Standards

- 7: Writing, Standard 1: Write arguments to support claims with clear reasons and relevant evidence. a. Introduce claim(s), acknowledge alternate or opposing claims, and organize the reasons and evidence logically. b. Support claim(s) with logical reasoning and relevant evidence, using accurate, credible sources and demonstrating an understanding of the topic or text.

- 8: Writing, Standard 1: Write arguments to support claims with clear reasons and relevant evidence. a. Introduce claim(s), acknowledge and distinguish the claim(s) from alternate or opposing claims, and organize the reasons and evidence logically. b. Support claim(s) with logical reasoning and relevant evidence, using accurate, credible sources and demonstrating an understanding of the topic or text.

Objectives

- Students will support claims with clear reasons and relevant evidence to craft fair, well-supported arguments.

- Students will organize reasons, evidence, and response to opposing claims logically in written arguments.

Background Knowledge Required

Students should have gathered their evidence at this point and be tying it into their essays.

Materials Needed

- Students should have their evidence/essay notes with them.

- Copies of the handout: Argument Map, p. 96

Agenda

1. **Introduction**: Give students these sample sentences (read them or display them on a board):

   a. I really want to go to basketball camp. It would make me an awesome player.

   b. I really want to go to basketball camp. It would make me an awesome player. I understand that you're concerned about how much it costs, but I can earn the money to pay for it before camp starts.

   c. I really want to go to basketball camp. It would make me an awesome player. I understand that you're concerned about how much it costs, but it's just dumb to let money rule your life like that!

   Have students vote on which one is the most convincing. Ask them to justify their votes. Discuss what makes the second argument the most convincing (not length). It's effective because it doesn't ignore the other person's argument; it addresses the opposing argument and points out why it is invalid. An argument also needs to be fair—just insulting another person (argument three) makes an opposing argument less fair and therefore less convincing.

2. **Independent Work**: Have students look at the research they gathered and the evidence they have to support their arguments. Ask students to make T-charts listing possible opposing claims on the left and ways to address those claims on the right.

3. **Partner Work**: Pair each student with a partner. The writer of the T-chart reads the refutations of the opposing claims (the column on the right), and the partner looks for holes in the writer's thinking. Then the students switch roles and repeat the exercise.

4. **Activity**: Ask students to use their prewriting work to complete the handout.

5. **Wrap-Up**: Have students incorporate their work from the lesson into their essay drafts. Students should write one or two sentences explaining how they strengthened their writing and submit them to you. Alternatively, students could read their sentences to a small group or share them in the full class.

Extend the Lesson

- Ask students to exchange drafts with a partner. Pass out copies of the 4-point rubric that follows. Ask students to read their partners' drafts carefully and to score them based on the rubric. After that, students should meet with their partners to discuss and explain how they arrived at the scores.

- You can also have students find additional examples of concession-refutation in local newspapers.

Differentiation

For students who need extra support

- Have students write argumentative paragraphs with one or two reasons and evidence before they do full essays; that will give them more practice in describing evidence.

- Give students extra copies of the handout so they can try out more than one plan for their essays.

For advanced students

- Require that students include at least four reasons with evidence for each reason and also point out two opposing claims.

- Give students extra copies of the handout. Encourage them to make two plans for their essays and then identify the stronger of the two.

Assessment

- Monitor students as they complete the partner work. Check to make sure that each T-chart has two or three opposing claims with corresponding responses/refutations. If students are having a hard time finding holes in their partners' thinking, suggest that they instead explain why the response/refutation is so strong that they can't find holes.

- Evaluate students' work on the argument map, checking to make sure that students supplied valid information for each section of the map. Ask students to redo sections that are unclear, illogical, or insulting (in the case of addressing an opposing claim).

- Use the following rubric to evaluate students' essay drafts.

Score 4.0	The student • Introduces a claim about the topic. • Includes at least three reasons or pieces of evidence to support the claim. • Acknowledges alternative or opposing claims. No major errors or omissions in the score 4.0 content.
Score 3.5	The student demonstrates success at the 3.0 level plus partial success at the 4.0 level.
Score 3.0	The student • Introduces a claim about the topic. • Includes one or two reasons or pieces of evidence to support the claim. • Acknowledges alternative or opposing claims but in an unfair or illogical way (e.g., by insulting the opposition or by acknowledging an irrelevant claim). No major errors or omissions in the score 3.0 content.
Score 2.5	The student demonstrates success at the 2.0 level plus partial success at the 3.0 level.
Score 2.0	The student • Introduces a claim about the topic. • Includes one or two reasons or pieces of evidence to support the claim. No major errors or omissions in the score 2.0 content.

Score 1.5	The student demonstrates partial success at the 2.0 level; the student's claim may be implied rather than stated; the supporting reasons may be only loosely related to the topic.
Score 1.0	With help, the student achieves partial success at score 2.0 and 3.0 contents.
Score 0.5	With help, the student achieves partial success at score 2.0 content but not score 3.0 content.
Score 0.0	Even with help, the student has no success.

Additional Resources

This page from ReadWriteThink offers a detailed 4-point rubric for evaluating persuasive writing: www.readwritethink.org/files/resources/printouts/Persuasion%20Rubric.pdf. It is titled Persuasion Rubric but applies well to argument writing.

Notes

After implementing the lesson, reflect on what worked and what you would change the next time.

_____

_____

_____

_____

Name: _____   Date: _____

Argument Map

Topic: _____

Introduce your claim:	
Supporting reason 1:	Evidence (facts or examples) to support reason 1:
Supporting reason 2:	Evidence (facts or examples) to support reason 2:
Supporting reason 3:	Evidence (facts or examples) to support reason 3:
Opposing claim:	Response to opposing claim:
Conclusion:	

Speaking and Listening

Part 3

Overview

The days of having students give presentations with index cards are over. Students need practice using technology when they present, as they will be required to do in college and careers. They should "make strategic use of digital media and visual displays of data to express information and enhance understanding of presentations" (Common Core State Standards, p. 48). The standards also require students to engage in a variety of small- and large-group discussions. Students must learn how to listen and respond to one another effectively and how to disagree respectfully and build from one another's ideas. For more suggestions on teaching speaking and listening, read the checklist below.

Planning Checklist

When planning a CCSS-based speaking and listening lesson, remember these tips:

☐ Provide opportunities for students to read aloud so they can develop fluency and practice adjusting the pace, accuracy, tone, and stress with which they read.

☐ Students should deliver presentations for a variety of purposes. They should incorporate media and visuals into their presentations and make sure that their content and language are appropriate for their particular audience.

☐ Teach listening skills by having students listen to audio or film versions of texts. Students should compare what they gain from reading a text to what they gain from hearing the audio or film version. Students should also listen to speeches and evaluate the speakers' points of view and use of rhetoric and evidence.

☐ Make sure that you begin text-based class discussions by having students look closely at the words and language. Don't jump too quickly into broad or opinion-based questions until you're sure that students have a clear understanding of the work itself. The authors of the Common Core explain that an effective discussion starts with focused questions.

> An effective set of discussion questions might begin with relatively simple questions requiring attention to specific words, details, and arguments and then move on to explore the impact of those specifics on the text as a whole. Good questions will often linger over specific phrases and sentences to ensure careful

comprehension and also promote deep thinking and substantive analysis of the text. . . . Often, curricula surrounding texts leap too quickly into broad and wide-open questions of interpretation before cultivating command of the details and specific ideas in the text. (Coleman and Pimentel, pp. 7–10)

☐ Lead (and have students lead) substantive discussions in which students have to respond to peers, paraphrase what was said, ask for clarification, and revise their own ideas if necessary. Make sure your discussions don't consist of just "teacher asks, student answers, teacher asks, student answers." But don't assume that students already know how to respond effectively to one another. Spend time explicitly teaching speaking and listening skills. See the following strategies.

Strategies for Teaching Speaking and Listening Skills

- Model speaking and listening. For example, show that when you listen, you might make eye contact or nod. You might also summarize what the person ahead of you said before jumping into your own point.

- Have students set goals before a discussion and assess themselves after. For example, goals might include "speak at least three times," "agree or disagree with someone else in detail," "ask a question," and "keep an open mind" (Roberts and Billings, 2012, p. 21).

- Keep a map of students' talk turns so you can identify patterns. Roberts and Billings suggest having students sit in a circle during a discussion. Draw the seating pattern on a piece of paper (draw a circle and write students' names around it to show where they're sitting). During the discussion, draw arrows on the circle and take notes to keep track of who is responding to whom. This will help you see which sets of friends respond only to one another, which students rarely participate, etc.

- Record class discussions, and show the DVD to students afterward. This will help them be aware of their own habits. For example, students who "hog" the conversation might not realize that they do so.

- Use a variety of group formats so students have practice speaking in small and large groups.

- Teach students to respond to the text during a discussion. You might wish to start with a short passage in which the lines are numbered. Require students to cite a line number and/or phrase as evidence when they respond. Eventually, students won't need as many supports and will be able to have high-level discussions on their own.

Lesson Plans at a Glance

Yield or Jump In?

Creating Balanced Class Discussions

Grade Levels: 6–8

Time Frame: Approximately one class period

Overview: In this lesson, students will learn how to share talk turns so that everyone in the class can contribute meaningfully to academic discussions. Students will also learn how to disagree and agree respectfully. This lesson should be done early in the school year because it will set the tone for the rest of the year.

Common Core State Standards

- 6–8: Speaking and Listening, Standard 1: Engage effectively in a range of collaborative discussions . . . with diverse partners . . . building on others' ideas and expressing their own clearly.

- 6: Speaking and Listening, Standard 1c: Pose and respond to specific questions with elaboration and detail by making comments that contribute to the topic, text, or issue under discussion.

Objectives

- Students will examine how they contribute to class discussions and how they need to modify their sharing style.

- Students will recognize when to speak up more, listen more closely, yield to others more, and disagree respectfully during discussions.

Background Knowledge Required

No particular background knowledge is required for this lesson.

Materials Needed

- Copies of the handout: What's My Discussion Style? on p. 103

Agenda

1. **Introduction**: Tell students that today's lesson is a chance for them to think about how they will be learning and working together as a class for the rest of the year. Ask students how and why it can be useful to discuss a text with others vs. thinking about it independently. Write their responses on the board. (Possible answers—it's possible to learn something new from other people, it's good to get a variety of perspectives, it teaches you to respect other people's opinions, etc.)

2. **Activity**: Tell students that everyone has a different way of participating in class discussions. (If you were quiet or too talkative when you were your students' age, share that!) Ask them to fill out the survey on the handout. Collect the handouts, and tell students that only you will read their responses.

3. **Mini-Lesson: Speaking Skills**

    Speaking Up: Go over some tips that will help reluctant students speak up in class. For example, jotting down an answer before saying it sometimes helps. Tell students to keep paper available during discussions in case they want to jot anything down before sharing. Also remind them that there are no wrong answers and that a person who doesn't have any bad ideas doesn't have enough ideas!

    Yielding to Others: Go over some tips for sharing talk turns. For example, tell students to be aware of the balance during a discussion. If a student is answering a majority of the questions, that person should yield to others more.

    Disagreeing: Go over the importance of disagreeing. It is helpful to hear a variety of perspectives, but students should disagree respectfully.

    Listening: Review listening skills. Explain the importance of acknowledging listening by nodding when someone is speaking and looking at him or her and by summarizing what someone says when responding rather than abruptly moving on to a new topic.

4. **Practice**: Give a sample opinion, and have students practice how they would disagree. For example, dogs are better pets than cats. Have students raise their hands and give their opinions by addressing what the person who spoke before them said. Students can do this as a full class and with partners. Give students different prompts, and have them practice with different partners. Prompts should be simple; the point is just to practice responding and not to worry about answers for now. Explain to students that carrying on an effective discussion is a skill, and you don't expect them to be great at it right away. But, as they pointed out themselves early in the lesson, there are many benefits to discussing ideas with others, so it is a skill worth practicing.

5. **Wrap-Up**: Ask students to write brief paragraphs on what they learned about themselves from this lesson and what they will work on in the future. This can be done in class or for homework.

6. **If Time Remains**: Ask students to think about discussion formats. When is it good to work with partners? In small groups? In full groups? Explain that they will be doing all three throughout the year. Asking students to reflect on teaching methods helps them feel more in control of their own learning and more invested in the class.

Extend the Lesson

- Do a follow-up lesson on how to refer to the text when the class discussion revolves around literature. Explain the importance of using evidence in responses. Have students practice this skill.

Differentiation

For students who need extra support

- Spend more time on each discussion skill. Do more modeling (by practicing with one student in front of the whole class) before organizing the class into pairs. You may also wish to provide sentence starters to help students respond to one another. Here are some sample sentence starters from *'Tween Crayons and Curfews: Tips for Middle School Teachers* (2011), by Heather Wolpert-Gawron.

  > "I realize not everyone will agree with me, but . . ."
  > "That's an interesting idea, but maybe . . ."
  > "I see it a little differently because . . ."
  > "I agree with what _____ said about . . ."
  > "I was wondering/thinking about that too." (p. 21)

For advanced students

- Have students practice acknowledging the previous person's comments, as this is an advanced skill that requires paraphrasing or summarizing. In other words, they don't just say, "Good point, Joe." They must respectfully clarify, verify, or challenge Joe's ideas.

Assessment

- Check whether students applied what they learned to the partner activity.

- Evaluate students' reflection paragraphs.

- You will continually assess this throughout the year as students gain more practice with discussions, and discussions become more complex.

Additional Resources

- *Teaching Critical Thinking: Using Seminars for 21st Century Literacy*, by Terry Roberts and Laura Billings (Eye On Education, 2012), focuses on the Paideia Seminar but includes great ideas for getting students to hold balanced discussions.

Notes

After implementing the lesson, reflect on what worked and what you would change the next time.

_____

_____

_____

_____

What's My Discussion Style?

For items 1–3a, circle the statements that best apply to you. Then complete item 4.

1. I always talk a lot during class discussions.

2. I speak up a lot only if I really like the topic of the discussion.

3. I am usually quiet during class discussions.
   If the answer is no, skip to question 4.
   If the answer is yes, answer question 3a.

3a. Choose one of the following:

   a. I am quiet during discussions because I don't know the answer.

   b. I know the answer, but I don't like speaking in front of groups.

   c. I think I know the answer, but I don't want to be wrong.

4. In the space below, write some goals for the next class discussion. (Questions to consider: If you speak up a lot, do you think you allow other people a chance to talk? If you don't speak up a lot, would anything make you comfortable speaking up more?)

Formalities Required?

Considering Audience When Making Language Choices

Grade Levels: 6–8

Time Frame: Approximately one class period

Overview: In this lesson, students will think critically about how language can and should be adjusted according to one's audience and purpose. This lesson should ideally be done toward the beginning of the year because it will help students with their upcoming speaking and writing projects.

Common Core State Standards
- 6–8: Speaking and Listening, Standard 6: Adapt speech to a variety of contexts and tasks, demonstrating command of formal English when indicated or appropriate.

- 6–8: Speaking and Listening, Standard 1: Engage effectively in a range of collaborative discussions . . . with diverse partners . . . building on others' ideas and expressing their own clearly.

- 6–8: Writing, Standard 4: Produce clear and coherent writing in which the development, organization, and style are appropriate to task, purpose, and audience.

Objectives
- Students will recognize their own language use for different situations in their personal lives and in school.

- Students will adapt their language according to audience and purpose.

Background Knowledge Required
No particular background knowledge is required for this lesson.

Materials Needed
- Index cards on the handout: Audience Index Cards, p. 107

Agenda
1. **Introduction**: Ask students to name some of the different forms in which they communicate in and outside of school. (Possible answers: through texts, tweets, Facebook, e-mails, in person, etc.) Ask: How does their writing style vary for each format? Are they more careful about spelling and punctuation with certain formats than with others?

2. **Group Activity**: Tell students that no form of communication is right or wrong but depends on context—a form has to be appropriate for the audience and for the situation. Organize students into groups of three. Give each group a set of index cards. Each group has to arrange the cards in order from least formal language required to most formal language required. Groups should share their decisions with the full class. Note that not every group has to agree, but they have to justify their decisions.

3. **Independent Work**: Have students write paragraphs describing something they did for fun recently. Have them write their paragraphs as e-mails and then as 140-character tweets. Ask volunteers to share their responses with the full class.

4. **Wrap-Up**: Ask students to write short responses about what they learned from the exercise and how that will apply to their speaking and writing throughout the year in your class.

Extend the Lesson

- You can contextualize the formal language register by asking students: How would you explain an incident if you were testifying in court? How would you explain it in writing to your parents? How would you explain it in writing to your innocent seven-year-old sister or cousin? How would you explain it to a friend who will find it hilarious?

- This lesson will come in handy throughout the year as students complete a variety of oral presentations and writing assignments. Make sure to discuss your language expectations for each project you assign, and don't always make them the same. Students need to learn to adjust their speaking and writing styles for different contexts.

Differentiation

For students who need extra support
- Provide more examples of how language changes for different contexts before asking students to do the index card activity.

For advanced students
- Instead of writing e-mails and tweets, students can write blog posts and Facebook status updates.

Assessment

- Evaluate whether students were able to justify their decisions during the index card activity.

- Read students' reflections to see if they are gaining an understanding of audience.

Additional Resources

- The following ReadWriteThink lesson explores appropriate language use: www .readwritethink.org/resources/resource-print.html?id=159.

Notes

After implementing the lesson, reflect on what worked and what you would change the next time.

_____

_____

_____

_____

Audience Index Cards

Note to teachers: Photocopy and cut out these index cards. Give one set to each group, as outlined in Lesson 22. Students should line them up from least formal language required to most formal language required. Note that some of these are subjective, but students must justify their choices.

tweeting about a celebrity's performance at the Grammys	talking to a friend on the basketball court at recess
updating your Facebook status	writing a thank-you note to your grandparents
e-mailing a parent asking to stay over at a friend's house	writing a speech to a group of scientists
writing an essay for school about characterization in *The Scarlet Letter*	writing a speech to a parent organization
writing a summer job application	e-mailing a friend about an activity at summer camp

Look at What I'm Saying!

Creating Engaging Presentations

Grade Level: 6 (see Overview for suggested adaptations for grades 7 and 8)

Time Frame: Approximately three or four class periods.

Overview: In this lesson, students research information on a topic and then create engaging presentations with visuals. Lesson Plan 24 helps students practice their speaking skills before delivering their presentations to their audience. This lesson focuses on writing and speaking to communicate information. You can adapt this lesson to grade 7 or 8 by assigning students a debatable topic and guiding them to use visuals for presenting information and clarifying and strengthening their claims about the topic.

Common Core State Standards

- 6: Writing, Standard 7: Conduct short research projects to answer a question, drawing on several sources and refocusing the inquiry when appropriate.

- 6: Writing, Standard 10: Write routinely over extended time frames (time for research, reflection, and revision) and shorter time frames (a single sitting or a day or two) for a range of discipline-specific tasks, purposes, and audiences.

- 6: Speaking and Listening, Standard 5: Include multimedia components (e.g., graphics, images, music, sound) and visual displays in presentations to clarify information.

- 6: Speaking and Listening, Standard 6: Adapt speech to a variety of contexts and tasks, demonstrating command of formal English when indicated or appropriate.

Objectives

- Students will research multiple sources to answer a question.

- Students will consider the benefits of adding visuals to a presentation and what those visuals should include.

- Students will create PowerPoint or Prezi presentations using their research.

Background Knowledge Required

Students should have prior experience conducting research.

Materials Needed

- Sample PowerPoint presentations (Free ones on a variety of topics are available online.)

- Computers with Internet connections for online research and PowerPoint or Prezi software

- Copies of the handout: PowerPoint/Prezi Activity Sheet, p. 112

Agenda

1. **Introduction**: Tell students that they've been asked to help a local library gear up for its summer youth program. Library staffers plan to offer a series of presentations to teach young people how to use technology for fun purposes. Allow students to choose a specific aspect of technology that they would like to research. Ask them to phrase their topics in the form of questions. Here are a few ideas to get them thinking: How do I program a digital camera to take a group shot with me in it? How do I create a mix CD (or an MP3 playlist)? How do I work the electronic scoreboard at the city sports field? Remind students that their questions need to be focused enough so that they can answer by explaining a process of five to seven steps.

2. **Lesson 1**: Students should gather information on their topics and take notes that they will turn into presentations. As a full class, brainstorm a list of reliable types of sources for different types of information (e.g., user's manuals, official product websites, online tutorials). Tell students to consult at least three different sources of information. Consulting multiple sources will help them find the clearest, most relevant information. It will also help students spot weak or erroneous sources (for example, all sources but one agree on the process).

3. **Lesson 2** (next class): Ask students how multimedia and visuals can help people understand and remember information. Write students' responses on the board. Tell students that they will be required to present their findings using PowerPoint (or Prezi) software with visuals. Mention the importance of using visuals that evoke comparisons or create metaphors, as opposed to reading word for word from the screen. Show students examples of successful and unsuccessful PowerPoints. Don't tell them which ones are good and which ones are bad; have students decide for themselves and explain their opinions. Then, as a class, decide on five qualities of an effective PowerPoint (or Prezi) presentation. Tell students they will have to incorporate those qualities into their presentations. Require about five to seven slides. Remind students to consider their audience—intelligent young people but perhaps with no background knowledge about the technical procedure. What needs to be defined, simplified, or clarified for this audience?

4. **Independent Work**: Have students review the information they gathered and decide how to express it using PowerPoint (or Prezi). Students should choose key steps in the technical procedures to list on the slides. They should also choose visuals that help explain the processes. Visuals might include diagrams, sketches, photographs, graphic organizers, and so on. Have students workshop their slide drafts with partners; they can help remove unnecessary information or add missing information to the slides. Remind students to add notes about what they might say as they're showing the slides. You should also walk around and provide feedback before students complete their final versions.

Extend the Lesson

- Pass out copies of the handout, and organize students into small groups. Each group should discuss the sample PowerPoints and their class notes to determine the qualities of an effective presentation. Students should fill in the handout to show how they think the slides of their presentations should be evaluated. Remind them that at this point, the slides themselves, not an oral presentation of the slides, will be evaluated. Have each group share its completed rubric with the full class.

Differentiation

For students who need extra support

- Provide more one-on-one support as they prepare their slides.

- Provide specific suggestions, either to individual students or via a list on the board, about what kinds of visuals to consider.

- Encourage students to review the examples of successful PowerPoint presentations after they complete the drafts of their own, looking for ways to improve their drafts.

For advanced students

- Allow students to include animation effects, such as animated clip art, and audio clips in their presentations.

- Ask volunteers to explain to the full class what part of their presentations they are most confident about.

- Ask questions and allow other students to ask questions, managing the discussion so that advanced students are acting as mentors to students who need extra support.

Assessment

- Check students' understanding of the reasons to add visuals to their presentations. Ask students to revise slides that are packed with too much visual information or too much text.

- Evaluate the handouts to see that students included key elements of an effective presentation in the top-score box, with the bullets in lower boxes showing a decrease in achievement of the key elements.

- Use the student-created rubrics or the following rubric to evaluate students' final drafts of their presentations.

Score 4.0	The student • Uses five to seven slides to explain a technical procedure. • Includes relevant visuals that make the procedure clear. • Includes words, phrases, or short sentences to help make the procedure clear, as needed. Text is clear and concise. No major errors or omissions in the score 4.0 content.
Score 3.5	The student demonstrates success at the 3.0 level plus partial success at the 4.0 level.

Score 3.0	The student • Uses four or fewer slides to explain a technical procedure. • Includes relevant visuals to help explain the procedure, though visuals may be too few or too crowded. • Includes words, phrases, or short sentences to help make the procedure clear, as needed. Text may need editing for clarity or conciseness. No major errors or omissions in the score 3.0 content.
Score 2.5	The student demonstrates success at the 2.0 level plus partial success at the 3.0 level.
Score 2.0	The student • Uses three or fewer slides to explain a technical procedure. • Includes visuals, though some are irrelevant, unclear, and/or too crowded. • Includes words, phrases, or short sentences, though text is unclear and/or overused. No major errors or omissions in the score 2.0 content.
Score 1.5	The student demonstrates partial success at the 2.0 level.
Score 1.0	With help, the student achieves partial success at score 2.0 and 3.0 contents.
Score 0.5	With help, the student achieves partial success at score 2.0 content but not score 3.0 content.
Score 0.0	Even with help, the student has no success.

Additional Resources

- Prezi can be found at prezi.com.

- Consult Mike Splane's "PowerPoint Presentation Advice" for additional tips to share with your students: www.cob.sjsu.edu/splane_m/PresentationTips.htm.

Notes

After implementing the lesson, reflect on what worked and what you would change the next time.

_____

_____

_____

_____

PowerPoint/Prezi Activity Sheet

A rubric is a detailed guide for evaluating or grading work. Complete the rubric below by filling in bullet items to show what makes an effective PowerPoint or Prezi presentation. A top-score presentation should effectively use the most important elements, or parts, of a PowerPoint or Prezi presentation. Lower scores may be missing important parts or may have errors in the important parts.

Score 4.0	The student ▪ ▪ ▪ No major errors or omissions in the score 4.0 content.
Score 3.5	The student demonstrates success at the 3.0 level plus partial success at the 4.0 level.
Score 3.0	The student ▪ ▪ ▪ No major errors or omissions in the score 3.0 content.
Score 2.5	The student demonstrates success at the 2.0 level plus partial success at the 3.0 level.
Score 2.0	The student ▪ ▪ ▪ No major errors or omissions in the score 2.0 content.
Score 1.5	The student demonstrates partial success at the 2.0 level.
Score 1.0	With help, the student achieves partial success at score 2.0 and 3.0 contents.
Score 0.5	With help, the student achieves partial success at score 2.0 content but not score 3.0 content.
Score 0.0	Even with help, the student has no success.

Please Lend Me an Ear

Presenting Your Findings

Grade Level: 6 (see Overview for adaptations for 7 and 8)

Time Frame: Approximately two or three class periods

Overview: Students will learn speaking skills required when delivering a formal presentation. This lesson immediately follows Lesson Plan 23 on page 108. If you adapted Lesson Plan 23 for grade 7 or 8, you can use this lesson in those grades.

Common Core State Standards

- 6: Speaking and Listening, Standard 1: Engage effectively in a range of collaborative discussions . . . with diverse partners on *grade 6 topics, texts, and issues*, building on others' ideas and expressing their own clearly. b. Follow rules for collegial discussions, set specific goals and deadlines, and define individual roles as needed.

- 6: Speaking and Listening, Standard 4: Present claims and findings, sequencing ideas logically and using pertinent descriptions, facts, and details to accentuate main ideas or themes; use appropriate eye contact, adequate volume, and clear pronunciation.

- 6: Speaking and Listening, Standard 5: Include multimedia components (e.g., graphics, images, music, sound) and visual displays in presentations to clarify information.

- 6: Speaking and Listening, Standard 6: Adapt speech to a variety of contexts and tasks, demonstrating command of formal English when indicated or appropriate.

Objectives

- Students will deliver a PowerPoint or Prezi presentation.

- Students will practice using eye contact, adequate speaking volume, and clear pronunciation during an oral presentation.

- Students will give one another collegial feedback on their presentations.

Background Knowledge Required

This lesson should be done after students create visual presentations on an assigned or a selected topic, such as the presentation created in Lesson Plan 23.

Materials Needed

- Students' PowerPoint or Prezi presentations

113

- Computers with PowerPoint or Prezi software

- Copies of the handout: Presentation Activity Sheet, p. 117

Agenda

1. **Introduction**: Tell students that they've worked really hard on creating engaging presentations, but engaging presentations need engaging presenters! Ask: What are the qualities of a good presenter? Write responses on the board. (They might include the following: Don't just read the slides; look at the audience, speak loudly and clearly, etc.)

2. **Teacher Modeling**: Read a short speech in a couple of different styles (without a lot of eye contact, too fast or too slowly, etc.) Have students comment on what is effective and what could be improved. Use this discussion as an opportunity to give students tips on how to give respectful, effective feedback. For example, comments (even given jokingly) such as "That's so lame!" or "You sound like a mouse" are not helpful. Comments such as "You started out speaking clearly, but then you started saying your words too fast" are more helpful. Remind students that public speaking can be nerve-racking even for professionals, but a supportive audience and peers who want to help someone improve can make all the difference.

3. **Partner Work**: Have students work with a partner to complete the rubric on page 117 for evaluating presentations.

4. **Practice**: Have students practice saying their presentations to partners. If time permits, have each student work with two different partners (one at a time) so that students can get two different perspectives. You could also have students record their partners' presentations so that students can listen to and watch themselves and see what they would like to improve. Students often aren't aware of their own habits unless they get a chance to see and hear them.

5. **Wrap-Up**: When students are done practicing, have them deliver their presentations to their real audience! If the audience is young people who are attending how-to sessions at a library, consider booking a community room at a library. Advertise the program to attract authentic attendees, and have students give their presentations in this venue.

Extend the Lesson

- Have students post their slides, or recordings of their live presentations, to a classroom website, a personal website, or a public website such as YouTube.

Differentiation

For students who need extra support

- Allow students more time to prepare their presentations. Help them one-on-one with any pronunciation issues or other concerns.

- Pair timid students with presentation-day buddies. The buddies will sit in the audience and provide encouragement via smiles, nods, or prepared handheld signs such as "Smile!" and "Great!"

For advanced students

- Have those students take on extra speaking roles. For example, they can emcee during the live presentations by introducing their classmates' presentations.

- Ask technologically skilled students to stand by on presentation day to help trouble-shoot the presentation software for their peers. Have one student on standby during each presentation, tasked with watching for signs of trouble. If the presenter is timid, ask a confident troubleshooter to stand just behind and to the side of the presenter so the timid person doesn't feel so alone in front of the audience.

Assessment

- Monitor students during the practice activity, listening for acceptable and unacceptable feedback. Take a break midway through the work period to give students examples of some of the respectful and disrespectful comments you have heard.

- Evaluate students' work on the handout to see that they included key elements of an effective presentation in the top-score box, with the bullets in lower boxes showing a decrease in achievement of the key elements.

- After the live presentations, ask students to write paragraphs evaluating their performances, noting strengths and what they would change next time.

- Use a student-created rubric or the following rubric to evaluate students' live presentations.

Score 4.0	The student • Speaks in a natural, unhurried voice. • Speaks loudly enough to be heard clearly in the back row. • Makes eye contact with each section of the audience (left, right, front, back). • Uses techniques such as repetition of key points and humor to engage the audience. • Answers questions clearly and concisely. No major errors or omissions in the score 4.0 content.
Score 3.5	The student demonstrates success at the 3.0 level plus partial success at the 4.0 level.
Score 3.0	The student • Speaks most of the time in a natural, unhurried voice. • Speaks most of the time in a clearly audible voice. • Makes some eye contact with the audience. • Attempts to engage the audience once or twice by repeating a key point or using humor (even if the audience doesn't laugh!). • Answers questions, though answers might be too brief or may ramble. No major errors or omissions in the score 3.0 content.
Score 2.5	The student demonstrates success at the 2.0 level plus partial success at the 3.0 level.

Score 2.0	The student • Speaks too quickly most of the time. • Speaks too loudly or too quietly most of the time. • Makes eye contact with the audience once or twice. • Answers questions, though answers might be too brief or may ramble. No major errors or omissions in the score 2.0 content.
Score 1.5	The student demonstrates partial success at the 2.0 level.
Score 1.0	With help, the student achieves partial success at score 2.0 and 3.0 contents.
Score 0.5	With help, the student achieves partial success at score 2.0 content but not score 3.0 content.
Score 0.0	Even with help, the student has no success.

Additional Resources

- This site has a good list of tips for effectively delivering a presentation: go.owu.edu/~dapeople/ggpresnt.html.

Notes

After implementing the lesson, reflect on what worked and what you would change the next time.

_____

_____

_____

_____

Name: _____   Date: _____

Presentation Activity Sheet

A rubric *is a detailed guide for evaluating or grading work. Complete the rubric below by filling in bullet items to show what makes an effective oral presentation. A top-score presentation should demonstrate key speaking skills. Lower scores demonstrate key skills only partly successfully or may leave out key skills.*

Score 4.0	The student ▪ ▪ ▪ No major errors or omissions in the score 4.0 content.
Score 3.5	The student demonstrates success at the 3.0 level plus partial success at the 4.0 level.
Score 3.0	The student ▪ ▪ ▪ No major errors or omissions in the score 3.0 content.
Score 2.5	The student demonstrates success at the 2.0 level plus partial success at the 3.0 level.
Score 2.0	The student ▪ ▪ ▪ No major errors or omissions in the score 2.0 content.
Score 1.5	The student demonstrates partial success at the 2.0 level.
Score 1.0	With help, the student achieves partial success at score 2.0 and 3.0 contents
Score 0.5	With help, the student achieves partial success at score 2.0 content but not score 3.0 content.
Score 0.0	Even with help, the student has no success.

There's Information at Your Fingertips, but Is It All Worthwhile?

Comparing Media Formats

Grade Levels: 6–8

Time Frame: Approximately one class period

Overview: This lesson teaches students to think critically about how (and why) information is presented in different media formats. The lesson uses the 2011 tsunami in Japan as the example, but you can pick a more recent current event so you can access the most resources possible. You may wish to pair up with a social studies teacher and do this lesson together.

Common Core State Standards

- 6: Speaking and Listening, Standard 2: Interpret information presented in diverse media and formats and explain how it contributes to a topic, text, or issue under study.

- 7: Speaking and Listening, Standard 2: Analyze the main ideas and supporting ideas presented in diverse media and formats (e.g., visually, quantitatively, orally) and explain how the ideas clarify a topic, text, or issue under study.

- 8: Speaking and Listening, Standard 2: Analyze the purpose of information presented in diverse media and formats (e.g., visually, quantitatively, orally) and evaluate the motives (e.g., social, commercial, political) behind its presentation.

Objectives

- Students will analyze the benefits and drawbacks of different media formats to communicate news and ideas.

- Students will select an appropriate media format for an assigned topic.

Background Knowledge Required

No particular background knowledge is required for this lesson.

Materials Needed

- Copies of Different Forms of Media, p. 121. The handout uses a table format. You can also use a matrix graphic organizer to help students see points of comparison among various sources.

- Sources of information about the 2011 tsunami, including audio and video clips

Agenda

1. **Introduction**: Ask students to name the first source they would use to find out about a world event, such as the tsunami in Japan. (Possible answers: a parent, the Yahoo homepage when checking e-mail, news at night while watching TV, etc.). Give students the media handout. Have them complete only the left-hand column for now. They should describe how each form of media might cover the news differently.

2. **Mini-Lesson**: Introduce a current event, such as the Japanese tsunami of 2011. Present students with a bunch of different resources, one by one. Resources should include audio clips, videos, magazine articles, photos, and charts. Discuss the differences among these resources in terms of information provided, emotional appeal, and ulterior motives (such as a political motive or a goal to sell magazines).

3. **Group Work**: Organize students into three groups. Assign one group the science of the tsunami, one group the effect it had on people's lives in Japan, and one group what the United States did to help. Each group has to decide what kinds of audio and visuals would be most appropriate for teaching this event to others and why.

4. **Wrap-Up**: Groups should share their decisions with the full class. They should also share what they learned about the benefits and drawbacks of different forms of media.

Extend the Lesson

- Have students conduct research on the topic assigned to their group. Each group should create a presentation in the media form(s) that they chose and share them with the class.

Differentiation

For students who need extra support

- Organize students into groups based on skill level so that you can spend more time with certain groups.

For advanced students

- Organize the groups so that struggling students are paired with more advanced students who can assist them.

Assessment

- Evaluate students' work in the group activity to see whether they thought critically about the different kinds of mediums and how they help disseminate information.

Additional Resources

- This chart lists different mediums and their benefits and drawbacks: 63.175.159.26/~cimh/cami/files/PUBCOMM/PresK11/PDF/Media%20Matrix.2.pdf. Have students pretend that they work for a company that sells a certain type of service or that promotes a cause. Ask them which media format they would use to spread the news about that service or cause.

Notes

After implementing the lesson, reflect on what worked and what you would change the next time.

_____

_____

_____

_____

Name: _____   Date: _____

Different Forms of Media

How might each of these types of media report the news differently? Add other possible media formats in the empty boxes below.

Medium	What I think before the lesson	What I think after the lesson
newspaper article		
magazine article		
photo slide show on news site		
TV newscast		
YouTube video		
a journalist's Twitter feed		
another source: _____		
another source: _____		

Language

Overview

The Common Core State Standards for language cover the full range of conventions in grammar, usage, capitalization, punctuation, and spelling. However, they don't advocate teaching the rules in isolation; they require teaching students how the rules *apply* to language, style, and meaning. They also emphasize the importance of teaching students to adjust their language based on audience and purpose. Students don't always have to write in a formal style "for the teacher"; they can also write in informal styles, but they should learn to decide *when* a particular style is most appropriate.

In addition to emphasizing grammar and style, the standards also stress vocabulary. Teach words explicitly and also implicitly through your own word choices. Don't require students to memorize words and use them in sentences; help students truly understand what the words mean by using them in different contexts and analyzing shades of meaning. Focus on academic vocabulary, which is essential to students' success in school and beyond. Give students tools to uncover word meanings on their own so they can become more independent readers and writers. Following is a list of other key points to keep in mind when designing language lessons.

Planning Checklist

When planning a CCSS-based language lesson, remember these tips:

☐ Teach students grammar and conventions, and make sure that each year builds on the previous year. Students need to gain "mastery of the full range of grammar and conventions as they are applied in increasingly sophisticated contexts" (Coleman and Pimentel, p. 13).

☐ Help students understand language "as a matter of craft" and learn when it is necessary to use standard written and spoken English (Coleman and Pimentel, p. 13). Students need to learn to make effective language choices on their own, based on their audience and purpose.

☐ Give English language learners extra support (as necessary) with academic language. ELLs often pick up social language quickly but have a more difficult time with Tier Two academic words.

☐ Show students how to think critically about words when writing or analyzing an author's choices. Students should consider nuances in word meanings, figurative language, and connotations of words.

☐ Teach academic (Tier Two) words implicitly and explicitly. Also teach domain-specific (Tier Three) words. Following are some strategies for teaching vocabulary.

Strategies for Teaching Vocabulary

- Teach context clues and when not to use them. Sometimes, it is necessary to consult a reference source to confirm a guess or find a meaning.

- Teach Greek and Latin affixes. This will help students expand their word knowledge and determine the meanings of unknown words.

- Choose relevant, academic vocabulary words to teach rather than the esoteric words of a novel.

- Don't have students memorize word lists and use them in sentences. Students will learn the words for a quiz and forget them days later. Have students explore the words in more depth, such as by relating the words to their own contexts and to other words they know. Benjamin and Crow (2013) provide the following example of how to engage students in vocabulary instruction:

  > An example of a meaningful engagement would be for students to create a blog about a topic of interest and carry on an online conversation that is laced with target words. Even if the target words do sound forced, at least the student is combing through the new vocabulary in search of words that actually communicate their ideas. (p. 117)

- Inspire word curiosity among students. Debbie Arechiga (2012) recommends having a word collector jar. Every day, students submit interesting words they have heard or seen. The teacher will often "select a word from the jar, write it on the board, display it in a meaningful sentence, and then invite discussion about the word's meaning and connection to their lives" (p. 170).

Lesson Plans at a Glance

The Case of the Missing Pronoun

Grade Level: 6 (see Overview for adaptations for grades 7 and 8)

Time Frame: Approximately two or three class periods

Overview: In the Common Core, grade 1 students begin learning to use pronouns and, in successive years, to understand their purposes in sentences. Grade 6 is the first year in which students are asked to focus on correcting errors in pronoun usage. This lesson teaches students to recognize and correct common errors. You can use this lesson for grades 7 and 8 as well because the Common Core encourages students in grades 7 and higher to further develop their skills and understanding of correct pronoun usage.

Common Core State Standards

- 6: Language, Standard 1: Demonstrate command of the conventions of standard English grammar and usage when writing or speaking. a. Ensure that pronouns are in the proper case (subjective, objective, possessive). b. Use intensive pronouns (e.g., *myself, ourselves*). c. Recognize and correct inappropriate shifts in pronoun number and person. d. Recognize and correct vague pronouns (i.e., ones with unclear or ambiguous antecedents).
- 6: Writing, Standard 5: With some guidance and support from peers and adults, develop and strengthen writing as needed by planning, revising, editing, rewriting, or trying a new approach.

Objectives

- Students will learn to recognize and correct common errors in pronoun usage, in their own and others' writing.

Background Knowledge Required

Students should know how to identify pronouns in sentences from their work in earlier grades.

Materials Needed

- Copies of the handout: Pronoun Activity Sheet, p. 130

- Drafts of writing that students are working on. The day before you teach the lesson, remind students to bring their drafts to class.

Agenda

1. **Introduction**: Ask students to take out a piece of writing that they have been working on, either for this or another class. Tell them to skim their writing to find sentences that use pronouns. While they do that, draw an empty chart on the board, such as this one.

Personal Pronouns

	Singular	Plural
Subjective		
Possessive		
Objective		

Ask a volunteer to read aloud a sentence that uses a pronoun. Have the student identify the pronoun. Repeat the process a number of times, each time writing the pronoun in the appropriate space in the chart on the board. After a few minutes, tell students that you will fill in the rest of the pronouns in the chart. It should look like this.

Personal Pronouns

	Singular	Plural
Subjective	I you he, she, it	we you they
Possessive	my, mine your, yours his, hers, its	our, ours your, yours their, theirs
Objective	me you him, her, it	us you them

Explain briefly that subjective case pronouns work as subjects in sentences. Possessive case pronouns show ownership in sentences. Objective case pronouns work as objects of verbs or prepositions in sentences.

Tell students that, as they know, certain rules guide the use of pronouns in sentences. Most of the time, people use pronouns correctly, but sometimes they make mistakes. Some common errors are these:

Using a pronoun in the wrong case:
Incorrect: At the concert, Willow sat between Sam and I.
Correct: At the concert, Willow sat between Sam and me.
Incorrect: The singer greeted them and myself.
Correct: The singer greeted them and me. (Like *them, me* is in the objective case. They are objects of the verb *greeted*. Give students this tip: If you're not sure whether to use *I* or *me*, take the other person out of the equation. You would say, "The singer greeted me," not "The singer greeted I"; therefore you also say, "The singer greeted them and me.")
Correct: I myself got to meet the singer. (Here is an example of the correct use of an intensive pronoun such as *myself, yourself,* and *ourselves*. An intensive pronoun adds emphasis to the pronoun that it immediately follows.)

Making an incorrect shift in pronoun number or person:
Incorrect: Someone left their jacket behind on the bleachers. (*Someone* is singular, but *their* is plural.)
Correct: Someone left his or her jacket behind on the bleachers.
Incorrect: He scanned the horizon for storm clouds. You don't want to get caught in a storm far from shore. (The first sentence uses third person. The second sentence shifts to second person.)
Correct: He scanned the horizon for storm clouds. He didn't want to get caught in a storm far from shore. (The verb had to be revised to agree with the pronoun *he*.)

Using pronouns that are confusing because it is unclear what the antecedent is:
Incorrect: When Princess saw Queenie, she wagged her tail happily. (Who wagged her tail—Princess or Queenie?)
Correct: When Princess saw Queenie, Princess wagged her tail happily.
Correct: Princess wagged her tail happily when she saw Queenie.

2. **Small-Group Activity**: Distribute the handout. Organize students into pairs or threes to complete it.

3. **Full-Class Activity**: Go over the handout as a full class. Call on individuals or groups to share their answers to items on the handout. If more than one correction is possible, as in items 14 and 15, explain that sometimes there is more than one way to correct a mistake.

4. **Wrap-Up**: For homework, have students revise pieces of their own writing for errors in pronoun usage.

Differentiation

For students who need extra support

▪ Monitor these students more closely during the small-group activity, providing tips and affirmation to help them make progress. Extend the lesson to include an additional class period.

- Provide a handout that you create, modeled on the handout in this lesson. Reinforce the rules of pronoun usage as you guide students through the correction of each error.

For advanced students

- Ask volunteers to write sentences with errors on the board, and guide the class through the identification and correction of the errors. Students may draw on sentences from their own writing.

Assessment

- Monitor students during the small-group activity, making sure that each student is participating. If a number of groups are struggling, ask groups to stop where they are. Complete the handout as a full class.

- Check the revisions that students made to their own pieces of writing to see that the revised drafts demonstrate command of correct pronoun usage. If a number of students are still struggling, have them workshop a paragraph or two of their writing with partners during class time.

Additional Resources

- Purdue's OWL site has informative sections on pronoun case and using pronouns clearly: owl.english.purdue.edu/owl/resource/595/1.

- You can find numerous worksheets on pronoun agreement (in number and person), pronoun case, and pronoun reference at Grammar Bytes!: www.chompchomp.com/handouts.htm.

Notes

After implementing the lesson, reflect on what worked and what you would change next time.

_____

_____

_____

_____

Name: _____   Date: _____

Pronoun Activity Sheet

Thirteen of the sentences below have one error in the use of a pronoun. Cross out each error, and write a correction above it. Two sentences have a blank. Complete the sentences by writing an intensive pronoun in each blank.

1. Everyone has a hobby, and spending time on this activity can make you happy.

2. Looking at the entries in the art show, the judge was impressed by their talent.

3. If I tell you a secret, can you keep it between you and I?

4. Caroline and myself are planning an end-of-year party for our friends.

5. If you ride your skateboard inside the mall, they will make you leave the building.

6. Either Zach Harris or Derek Dunson will lend me their inflatable raft.

7. Kirby and them are planning a backyard dance party.

8. I saw they house and I said to myself, "Oh, wow! It's a log cabin!"

9. You _____ hold the key to your destiny.

10. If you trespass on private property, they can call the police.

11. Each student should write their name on the front of the test booklet.

12. Them are hot chili peppers, so don't take a huge bite of one!

13. I wondered who had made Fiona angry; it turned out that I _____ had hurt her feelings with a careless comment.

14. Rosa told Ava that she had made a perfect score on the math test.

15. After baseball practice, Joseph and Eric looked at his collection of baseball cards.

Answer key for Pronoun Activity Sheet

Grade 6 Language Standard Correlation	Corrected Item
1. c.	1. Everyone has a hobby, and spending time on this activity can make ~~you~~ <u>him or her</u> happy.
1. d.	2. Looking at the entries in the art show, the judge was impressed by ~~their~~ <u>the artists'</u> talent.
1. a.	3. If I tell you a secret, can you keep it between you and ~~I~~ <u>me</u>?
1. a.	4. Caroline and ~~myself~~ <u>I</u> are planning an end-of-year party for our friends.
1. d.	5. If you ride your skateboard inside the mall, ~~they~~ <u>a security guard</u> will make you leave the building.
1. c.	6. Either Zach Harris or Derek Dunson will lend me ~~their~~ <u>his</u> inflatable raft.
1. a.	7. Kirby and ~~them~~ <u>they</u> are planning a backyard dance party.
1. a.	8. I saw ~~they~~ <u>their</u> house and I said to myself, "Oh, wow! It's a log cabin!"
1. b.	9. You ___<u>yourself</u>___ hold the key to your destiny.
1. d.	10. If you trespass on private property, ~~they~~ <u>the owners</u> can call the police.
1. c.	11. Each student should write ~~their~~ <u>his or her</u> name on the front of the test booklet.
1. a.	12. ~~Them~~ <u>They</u> are hot chili peppers, so don't take a huge bite of one!
1. b.	13. I wondered who had made Fiona angry; it turned out that I ___<u>myself</u>___ had hurt her feelings with a careless comment.
1. d.	14. Rosa told Ava that ~~she~~ <u>Rosa (OR Ava)</u> had made a perfect score on the math test. *Note: Explain that a complete revision of this type of error can produce a more polished sentence. In the following example, it is clear that the pronoun* she *refers to Rosa, not Ava.* *When Rosa saw the perfect score on her math test, she told Ava.*
1. d.	15. After baseball practice, Joseph and Eric looked at his <u>Joseph's (OR Eric's)</u> collection of baseball cards. *Note: As with sentence 14, this sentence can be revised to create a more polished sentence. Here is an example:* *After baseball practice, Eric showed his collection of baseball cards to Joseph.*

What's the Right Context for Context Clues?

Grade Levels: 6–8

Time Frame: Approximately one class period

Overview: The following lesson teaches students to think critically about the decisions they have to make as readers when they come across unknown words. This lesson is done with a literary text but can also be done with informational texts. You can consult with content area teachers to find out what students are reading in those classes and then apply this lesson to those texts.

Common Core State Standards

- 6–8: Language, Standard 4: Determine or clarify the meaning of unknown and multiple-meaning words and phrases . . . choosing flexibly from a range of strategies.

- 6–8: Reading, Literature, Standard 4: Determine the meaning of words and phrases as they are used in the text, including figurative and connotative meanings.

Objectives

- Students will learn about the different types of context clues and how they help readers.

- Students will learn what to do when they come across an unknown word—when to use context clues and when to look up a word in the dictionary.

Background Knowledge Required

No particular background knowledge is required for this lesson.

Materials Needed

- Copies of the handout: Common Types of Context Clues, p. 135

- Excerpt from *The Invisible Man*, found on Google Books at http://tinyurl.com/cctawzg

Agenda

1. **Introduction**: Write two sentences on the board:

   a. I have a penchant for chocolate. I eat it almost every day.
   b. Joey acquiesced to his older brother's demands. What would you have done?

Ask students: "In which sentence can you figure out the meaning from context? Why/how?" (The answer is the first statement. The clue is in the second sentence.)

2. **Lesson**: Teach the different types of clues, and have students come up with their own examples using the handout on page 135. Explain that authors sometimes give context clues, and sometimes they don't. Ask: What can readers do when they don't have context clues? (Possible answers: look a word up in a dictionary, keep reading anyway, ask someone, etc.) You should show students that readers don't look up every single word they don't know; they would get too bogged down and never finish or enjoy a book.

3. **Independent Work**: Give students a short story or story excerpt with some difficult words. For example, this lesson would work well with the first two paragraphs of Ralph Ellison's *The Invisible Man*, about why others refuse to see him. Students can make meaning of that section and relate to it without needing to read the rest of the novel. That excerpt contains rich ideas about identity. Have students circle words they don't know and figure them out from context or look them up if necessary.

4. **Wrap-Up**: Discuss the activity as a full class.

Extend the Lesson

- Have students write about or discuss the figurative uses of words in the Ellison excerpt, and discuss how his word choices contribute to the meaning and tone of the passage. (This meets the second half of the grade 6 Standard 4 for Reading Literature.)

- This lesson focuses on a few main types of context clues. Another main way to determine word meaning from context is to look at the word's affixes. Spend time on Latin and Greek roots and how to think about word parts when determining the meanings of unknown words.

Differentiation

For students who need extra support
- Spend more time on each kind of context clue, providing additional examples and having students come up with more examples from things they have read.

For advanced students
- Have them to read more of *The Invisible Man*, or give them a more challenging text.

Assessment

- Evaluate whether students were able to apply what they learned about context clues to the reading lesson.
- Check students' responses to the handout.

- You will continue to assess this throughout the year because students will need knowledge of context clues to become skilled readers.

Additional Resources

- ReadWriteThink has the following useful handout for teaching context clues: www .readwritethink.org/files/resources/lesson_images/lesson1089/types_context_clues.pdf.

Notes

After implementing the lesson, reflect on what worked and what you would change the next time.

_____

_____

_____

_____

Name: _____   Date: _____

Common Types of Context Clues

Read the types of context clues and the examples. Underline the context clue in each example. Then complete the third column by finding your own example for each.

Type of context clue	Example	Your own example from a text you are reading
Definition or restatement	I refused to acquiesce, or give in, to her unreasonable demands.	
Synonym	I have an aversion to sardines. I never eat them!	
Antonym	The teacher condoned Matthew's behavior. I don't agree with that; I would have punished him.	
Example	I was *ecstatic* when I heard the news. I couldn't stop jumping up and down for joy!	

Let's Figure Out Figurative Language

Grade Level: 6

Time Frame: Approximately one or two class periods

Overview: This lesson uses an excerpt from "The Remarkable Rocket," by Oscar Wilde, as the text, but you can modify the lesson to use any narrative that relies on personification. If you plan to extend the lesson to include similes and metaphors, check to make sure your text includes all three types of figurative language, or use separate texts for teaching each type. This particular text was chosen because, although the events of the narrative are simple, the language is rich and complex. The CCSS emphasize the importance of using language skills to decode meaning in complex texts.

Common Core State Standards
- 6: Language, Standard 5: Demonstrate understanding of figurative language, word relationships, and nuances in word meanings. a. Interpret figures of speech (e.g., personification) in context.

Objectives
- Students will identify and interpret figures of speech (personification, simile, metaphor) in the context of a narrative.

Background Knowledge Required
Students should be familiar with the terms *simile* and *metaphor* from earlier grades, although these terms will be reviewed in this lesson.

Materials Needed
- Copies of an excerpt from "The Remarkable Rocket." The complete story may be found at classiclit.about.com/library/bl-etexts/owilde/bl-owilde-rock.htm. Begin the excerpt about halfway through the story, with the paragraph beginning, "'It is not comfortable here,' he remarked . . ." Include 20 paragraphs, through the paragraph beginning, "'I don't think much of that,' said the Duck . . .'"
- Copies of the handout: Personification Activity Sheet, p. 139
- Copies of the handout: Simile and Metaphor Activity Sheet, p. 140

Agenda

1. **Introduction**: Create an idea web on the board. Write *personification in fairy tales* in the center. On connecting spokes, write types of animals that speak in traditional fairy tales, such as pigs, wolf, bears, and mice. Ask volunteers to tell the class about fairy tales that have one or more of these animals as characters. Examples may include "The Three Little Pigs," "Goldilocks and the Three Bears," "Cinderella," and so on. Refer to students' examples (talking pigs, mice that can sew clothes) to explain that authors often use the technique of personification. Personification is the giving of human qualities to animals, things, or ideas. Connect a spoke to each type of animal on the idea web, and write an example of personification, such as speaking or sleeping in beds. Tell students that with their knowledge of personification in fairy tales, they are prepared to spot personification in other stories too.

2. **Lesson**: Pass out copies of the excerpt. Introduce it by telling students that the main character is Rocket, who is a firework. He is eager to be fired into the air to celebrate the wedding of the king's son. Unfortunately, no one sets off Rocket. When the cleaning crew comes, someone tosses Rocket into a ditch. Point out that a talking firework is an example of personification. Ask students to listen and follow along on their own copies as you read the excerpt aloud. As you read, students should circle the name of each story character that provides an example of personification.

3. **Small-Group Activity**: After you finish reading, have students work in pairs to complete the handout.

4. **Wrap-Up**: Have students share with the class their work on the handout. Ask them to add additional ideas to their handouts as they listen to others' notes and ideas. Ask: "How does this author use personification to help his characters come alive for readers?" and "How would this story be different if all the characters were people?"

Extend the Lesson

- Briefly review similes and metaphors as forms of figurative language. Ask students to read the excerpt and underline each example of a simile or metaphor. (Three similes are in the last paragraph of the excerpt: "plough the fields like the ox," etc. A metaphor is in paragraph seven of the excerpt: "He is a perfect monster."). Have students use the excerpt from "The Remarkable Rocket" to complete the Simile and Metaphor Activity Sheet, either independently or in pairs. Ask students to share their notes and ideas in a full-class discussion.

- Have students work independently or with partners to find examples of personification in a narrative of their choosing. Suggested works include *Charlotte's Web* and *Stuart Little*, both by E. B. White, and *The Lion, The Witch, and the Wardrobe*, by C. S. Lewis. Each student or pair should use the chosen narrative to complete the Personification Activity Sheet. Ask students to share their notes and ideas in a full-class discussion.

Differentiation

For students who need extra support

- Pass out copies of the Personification Activity Sheet to use as a warm-up activity. Ask students to work with partners to complete the handout using information from a classic tale. Suggest that they use one of the fairy tales discussed in the lesson introduction or one of Aesop's fables. Have students share their notes and ideas in a full-class discussion.

- When assigning the Personification Activity Sheet as a small-group activity, first work as a class to complete the first row, using Rocket as the example.

- When extending the lesson to cover similes and metaphors, work as a class to complete the Simile and Metaphor Activity Sheet, using "The Remarkable Rocket." Ask students to write their own similes and metaphors and share them with the class.

For advanced students
- When extending the lesson to include similes and metaphors, have students read the entire text of "The Remarkable Rocket" to complete the Simile and Metaphor Activity Sheet.

Assessment
- Check students' handouts to verify that students understand how to identify personification in a story and why an author might use personification.

- If you extend the lesson to include similes and metaphors, check students' handouts to verify that students can identify similes and metaphors and can explain how the figurative language enhances the story.

Additional Resources
- An additional lesson plan for teaching personification is available here: teachers.net/lessons/posts/3509.html.http://teachers.net/lessons/posts/3509.html

Notes
After implementing the lesson, reflect on what worked and what you would change the next time.

_____

_____

_____

_____

Personification Activity Sheet

personification   a type of figurative language in which the writer gives human qualities to animals, things, or ideas. Examples: "The clouds wept" and "Love wrapped me in a hug."

Complete the following table. In the first column, write the names of characters who are not human but who show human qualities. In the middle column, identify what makes each character an example of personification. What human quality or qualities does the character have? In the third column, interpret the personification by completing the sentence starter.

Title of story or novel: _____		
Author: _____		
Name of Character	**Example(s) of Personification**	**This nonhuman character reminds me of the kind of person who . . .**

Name: _____ Date: _____

Simile and Metaphor Activity Sheet

simile   a type of figurative language in which the writer compares two things using the words *like* or *as*. Examples: "The old bread was as hard as a brick" and "His eyes were like blue swimming pools."

metaphor   a type of figurative language in which the writer compares two things by using a form of the verb *to be*. In other words, the writer states that one thing *is* another thing in order to make the reader notice how they are alike. For example, "The old bread was a brick" and "His eyes were blue swimming pools."

Complete the following table. In the first column, copy figures of speech that you identify in the story. In the second column, interpret each figure of speech by completing the sentence starter.

"The Remarkable Rocket" Author: Oscar Wilde	
Similes in the Story Copy each simile and underline the two things being compared.	**This simile helps me create a mental image of . . .**
Metaphors in the Story Copy each metaphor and underline the two things being compared.	**This metaphor helps me create a mental image of . . .**

Note: In some stories, you may find only one example of each type of figurative language. In other stories, you may find many examples. Use your own paper to record additional examples and response sentences, if necessary.

It's Not All Black and White

Understanding Shades of Meaning in Words

Grade Levels: 6–8

Time Frame: Approximately one class period

Overview: The following lesson teaches students about shades of meaning in words. Understanding nuances in word meanings will improve students' comprehension and help them make good decisions when writing.

Common Core State Standards

- 6–8: Language, Standard 5: Demonstrate understanding of figurative language, word relationships, and nuances in word meanings. c. Distinguish among the connotations (associations) or words with similar denotations (definitions).

- 6–8: Literature, Standard 4: Determine the meanings of words and phrases as they are used in a text, including figurative and connotative meanings.

Objectives

- Students will learn about shades of meaning and connotation.

- Students will practice thinking about connotation while reading and writing.

Background Knowledge Required

No particular background knowledge is required for this lesson.

Materials Needed

- Copies of the handout: Connotation and Denotation Graphic Organizer, p. 143

Agenda

1. **Introduction**: Write a few sets of close synonyms on the board, such as *dispute* and *argument, inquire* and *ask*, and *distinguished* and *famous*. Ask students to spend a few minutes jotting down the differences between the words.

2. **Mini-Lesson**: Have students share their responses with the full class. Point out that words have different shades of meaning and slightly different tones (informal or more formal, etc.) and that writers must think critically about what words they select when they write or think about what an author might mean when they read. Tell students that words also have feelings—they can have a positive or a negative

meaning. Write *denotation* and *connotation* on the board, and define them. Give students examples, and have them come up with some of their own examples.

3. **Partner Activity**: Distribute the handout. Have students go back over a short story or novel they've been reading in class. Have them select about five words and write the denotation and connotation of each.

4. **Wrap-Up**: Have students share their graphic organizers with the class.

Extend the Lesson

- You can have students do a writing exercise that consists of a passage with blanks. Have students fill in words with positive connotation. Then ask them to redo the exercise, using words with negative connotations. Discuss how the tone changes.

- Students can create short cartoons or videos (www.xtranormal.com is a good story-telling tool) to demonstrate their knowledge of connotation and denotation.

Differentiation

For students who need extra support
- Have them practice this activity with easier words before they apply it to a text they are reading.

For advanced students
- They can practice connotation and denotation with more advanced vocabulary words.

Assessment

- Check students' graphic organizers to see whether they were able to apply what they learned to something they are reading in class.

Additional Resources

- YourDictionary.com contains examples of connotative words and offers an exercise that students can complete: examples.yourdictionary.com/examples-of-connotative -words.html.

Notes

After implementing the lesson, reflect on what worked and what you would change the next time.

_____

_____

_____

_____

Connotation and Denotation Graphic Organizer

Word

_____

Denotation

_____

_____

_____

_____

Connotation

☐ Negative   ☐ Positive

Describe: _____

_____

_____

_____

_____

_____

Which Punctuation Mark Are You?

Grade Level: 6 (but can also be done as a review in grades 7 and 8)

Time Frame: Approximately one class period

Overview: This lesson teaches students about the function of punctuation. Students need to think critically about why authors use certain punctuation marks and learn to make decisions about what marks to use. This lesson should ideally be done toward the beginning of the year.

Common Core State Standards
- 6–8: Language, Standard 2: Demonstrate command of the conventions of standard English capitalization, punctuation, and spelling when writing.

- 6: Reading, Literature, Standard 6: Explain how an author develops the point of view of the narrator or speaker in a text.

- 6–8: Language, Standard 3: Use knowledge of language and its conventions when writing, speaking, reading, or listening.

Objectives
- Students will think critically about the role of punctuation in communicating content and tone.

Background Knowledge Required
Students should be familiar with a variety of basic punctuation marks.

Materials Needed
- Copies of the handout: How Punctuation Affects Tone, p. 147

Agenda
1. **Introduction**: Ask students to take a few minutes to think about their answer to this question: What punctuation mark are you? Ask: Are you an exclamation point because you're often excited when you tell stories? Are you a question mark because you have an inquisitive personality? Are you an ellipsis because you like to pause or leave out some details? Are you a period because you like to be very straightfor-ward? Have students share their answers, and don't forget to share your answer!

2. **Mini-Lesson**
   - How does punctuation affect meaning? Tell students that punctuation isn't just something that English teachers make them use; it affects meaning and tone. Write the following sentence on the board: Woman without her man is nothing. Have volunteers come up to the board and punctuate it. Options: Woman, without her man, is nothing. Woman! Without her, man is nothing. Explain how different (and insulting) these examples can be.
   - Here is another example: Please buy me strawberries ice cream and sugar. Without commas, the reader might think that the writer wants strawberries, ice cream, and sugar; however, the writer really wants strawberries, ice, cream, and sugar to make a special frozen dessert.
   - How does punctuation affect tone? Put the handout on an overhead or whiteboard. Show the two versions and have students read them aloud. How does punctuation affect the tone of each one?

3. **Independent Work**: Have students look at an excerpt from a novel or short story they are reading in class. Ask them to write short analyses of how the punctuation affects the tone and meaning in that passage and/or how it affects their view of the character. Discuss as a class.

Extend the Lesson
- Follow up on this lesson throughout the year. As students read literature and informational texts and analyze authors' decisions, remind them to consider punctuation as well as word choice.

Differentiation
For students who need extra support
- Give students a text with simpler sentence structures and punctuation to use for the independent work assignment.

For advanced students
- Give students a more challenging text to use for the independent work assignment.

Assessment
- Check that students are participating during the class discussion about punctuation and thinking critically about its role in communication.

- Evaluate students' analyses to see whether students were able to apply what they learned about punctuation to the text they are reading.

Additional Resources
- A good overview of punctuation rules is available on the Purdue Online Writing Lab site: owl.english.purdue.edu/owl/section/1/6/.

Notes

After implementing the lesson, reflect on what worked and what you would change the next time.

_____

_____

_____

_____

Name: _____   Date: _____

How Punctuation Affects Tone

As a class, read each paragraph aloud. Have more than one person read each version, following the punctuation. Then discuss the questions that follow.

Version 1

I'm really sorry that I stayed out past my curfew. I was having so much fun that I lost track of time. I wasn't doing anything bad—I was just watching a movie at Jenna's house. But I know I should have been more careful about the time, and I should have called you so you wouldn't worry. I promise that I will be more responsible next time.

Version 2

I'm really sorry that I stayed out past my curfew! I was having so much fun that I lost track of time! I wasn't doing anything bad!! I was just watching a movie at Jenna's house! But I know, I should have been more careful about the time . . . I should have called you so you wouldn't worry. I promise that I'll be more responsible next time!

Discussion Questions

Describe the tone of version 1.

Describe the tone of version 2. How is it different?

In which version does the speaker sound more genuinely apologetic?

In which version does the speaker sound more defensive?

In which version does the speaker sound more hysterical or worried about being punished? Does the speaker show more respect for his or her parent in one of the versions? Explain.

Choppy No More

Writing Compound Sentences to Link Ideas

Grade Levels: 6–7

Time Frame: Approximately one class period

Overview: This lesson teaches students how to form compound sentences. Ideally, students should do the lesson when they are working on a writing assignment (in English or for any subject) so they can apply what they learn about sentences to revise their drafts.

Common Core State Standards

- 6: Language, Standard 3: Use knowledge of language and its conventions when writing, speaking, reading, or listening. a. Vary sentence patterns for meaning, reader or listener interest, and style.

- 7: Language, Standard 1: Demonstrate command of the conventions of standard English grammar and usage when writing or speaking. b. Choose among simple, compound, complex, and compound-complex sentences to signal differing relationships among ideas.

- 6–7: Writing, Standard 5: With some guidance and support from peers and adults, develop and strengthen writing as needed by planning, revising, editing, rewriting, or trying a new approach.

Objectives

- Students will learn how to form a compound sentence.

- Students will use their knowledge of compound sentences to revise their essays for sentence variety.

Background Knowledge Required

Students should have a basic understanding of complete sentences versus fragments. They should be familiar with the terms *phrase* and *clause*; if not, review them before the lesson.

Materials Needed

- Copies of the handout: Using Compound Sentences to Link Ideas, p. 151

- Copies of a writing assignment that students are working on for this class or for another one

Agenda

1. **Introduction**: Put the paragraph from the handout on the board. Ask students what they think about the flow of sentences. Are there long and short sentences, or are they all the same length? How does that make the paragraph sound? (Answers: short, gives it a choppy feeling) How can we fix this?

2. **Mini-Lesson**: Show students two ways of combining simple sentences to form compound sentences—adding a coordinating conjunction (*and, or, but*) and a comma OR adding a semicolon. Make sure students understand what a simple sentence is. To help students remember that a semicolon doesn't need a coordinating conjunction, you can explain that it is strong enough on its own—it has upper body strength (the dot above the comma). Give students examples of both kinds of sentences based on the paragraph on the handout. Have students suggest ways to combine other sentences on the handout. Point out that the goal is for sentence variety, so the students don't want to combine *all* of them—they should leave some short ones in.

3. **Independent Work**: Have students go back to their essays and read them for sentence length. Which sentences could they combine? Have students make notes to use when writing their final drafts.

Extend the Lesson

- Have students check for sentence variety throughout the year as they complete writing assignments in your class.

- You can also have students identify compound sentences in a text they are reading.

Differentiation

For students who need extra support
- Have students workshop their essays with partners who can provide extra help.

For advanced students
- Have students incorporate complex sentences in addition to compound sentences.

Assessment

- Evaluate students' final essays for sentence variety. You can include sentence variety on the rubric you use to assess their final essays.

- Check students' participation during the class activity to see if they understand how sentence length affects the tone and flow of their writing.

Additional Resources

- Students can take this fun online quiz to check their knowledge of compound sentences: www.harcourtschool.com/activity/sentence_power/index.html.

Notes

After implementing the lesson, reflect on what worked and what you would change the next time.

_____

_____

_____

_____

Using Compound Sentences to Link Ideas

Read the following paragraph, which is made up of simple sentences. Combine some of the sentences into compound sentences. Then reread the passage to see how the flow changed.

Are you yawning at your desk right now? You are not alone. Many teenagers do not get enough sleep. They have a lot of homework to do. They watch TV and play on the computer late at night. Then they have to get up early for school. However, lack of sleep can make you cranky. It can affect your schoolwork. It is also bad for your health. It can run you down and make it hard to recover from a cold. Here are five tips for getting a better night's sleep, from WebMD's Teen Heath site:

1. Turn off your computer before you go to bed. You won't be distracted by e-mail alerts or the temptation to write back to someone.

2. If you have a lot on your mind before bedtime, you can play relaxing music. You can do yoga stretches.

3. Avoid caffeinated drinks in the evening.

4. Keep your room dark (close the shades if possible). Keep the temperature cool. It's harder to sleep when you are overheated.

5. If you're hungry before bed, eat crackers, pretzels, or cereal. The carbohydrates can help you feel sleepy. Have a snack. Don't have a full meal. A big meal is harder to digest and might keep you up.

Possible Answers to the Handout: Using Compound Sentences to Link Ideas

Are you yawning at your desk right now? You are not alone. Many teenagers do not get enough sleep. They have a lot of homework to do<u>, and</u> they watch TV and play on the computer late at night. Then they have to get up early for school. However, lack of sleep can make you cranky<u>, and</u> it can affect your schoolwork. It is also bad for your health. It can run you down and make it hard to recover from a cold. Here are five tips for getting a better night's sleep, from WebMD's Teen Heath site:

1. Turn off your computer before you go to bed<u>, so</u> you won't be distracted by e-mail alerts or the temptation to write back to someone.

2. If you have a lot on your mind before bedtime, you can play relaxing music<u>, or</u> you can do yoga stretches.

3. Avoid caffeinated drinks in the evening.

4. Keep your room dark (close the shades if possible)<u>, and</u> keep the temperature cool. It's harder to sleep when you are overheated.

5. If you're hungry before bed, eat crackers, pretzels, or cereal. The carbohydrates can help you feel sleepy. Have a snack<u>, but</u> don't have a full meal. A big meal is harder to digest and might keep you up.

Switch It Up!

Adding Complex Sentences to Your Writing

Grade Level: 7 (You can do this in grade 6 if your students have basic knowledge of sentence types. You can also do this in grade 8 as a review.)

Time Frame: Approximately one class period

Overview: This lesson shows students how to form complex and compound-complex sentences. Students will apply this lesson to a writing assignment they're working on for English or for another class.

Common Core State Standards

- 7: Language, Standard 1: Demonstrate command of the conventions of standard English grammar and usage when writing or speaking. b. Choose among simple, compound, complex, and compound-complex sentences to signal differing relationships among ideas.

- 7: Writing, Standard 5: With some guidance and support from peers and adults, develop and strengthen writing as needed by planning, revising, editing, rewriting, or trying a new approach.

Objectives

- Students will form complex and compound-complex sentences.

- Students will correctly punctuate compound and compound-complex sentences.

- Students will revise their essays for sentence variety.

Background Knowledge Required

Students should have prior knowledge of simple and compound sentences.

Materials Needed

- Copies of the handout, Using Complex Sentences to Link Ideas, p. 156

Agenda

1. **Introduction**: Ask students to remind you what they learned in the previous lesson about compound sentences. Explain that today, you're going to teach two other kinds of sentences: complex and compound-complex.

2. **Mini-Lesson**: Ask students what they think a complex sentence might be as opposed to a compound one. Then give them a formal definition with examples.

Don't forget to point out subordinating conjunctions and punctuation. Ask students how complex sentences link ideas differently than compound sentences do. Have them come up with some ideas: Ask: When would you use a complex sentence? Next, introduce compound-complex sentences (along with some examples), and repeat the process of having students identify when they might use them. Make sure students understand how to punctuate that type of sentence.

3. **Activity**: Display the sample paragraph (Using Complex Sentences to Link Ideas) on a board, and revise it as a class for compound, complex, and compound-complex sentences. (Give students hard copies of the handout to help them follow along.) Then read the new version against the old version and discuss how the flow has changed.

4. **Independent Work**: Have students use what they learned to revise something they wrote for class.

Extend the Lesson
- Have students identify different sentence types in something they're reading and discuss how the variety (or lack of variety) contributes to the flow of the text.

Differentiation
For students who need extra support
- Spend more time on each type of sentence.

- Have students workshop their essays with partners who can provide extra support.

For advanced students
- Students can find more examples of different types of sentences in a variety of informational and literary texts.

Assessment
- Evaluate whether students were able to revise their essays based on what they learned during the mini-lesson. You can include sentence variety on the rubric you use to assess their final essays. You can even require that students use at least one or two of each type of sentence they learned.

Additional Resources
- Students can check their knowledge of complex sentences with this fun online quiz: www.harcourtschool.com/activity/complex_sentence/index.html.

Notes

After implementing the lesson, reflect on what worked and what you would change the next time.

_____

_____

_____

_____

Using Complex Sentences to Link Ideas

Revise the passage below. Use compound, complex, and compound-complex sentences to link ideas and improve the flow of the paragraph.

Selena Gomez is a well-known actress. She began her career on *Barney and Friends*. Years later, she guest-starred on two shows. Those shows were *The Suite Life of Zack and Cody* and *Hannah Montana*. Then she got her big break. She landed the lead on *Wizards of Waverly Place*. She plays Alex. Selena is not just an actress. She is also a singer. She has two albums. She even designed a clothing line, Dream Out Loud. It is sold at Kmart. Selena is also well-known for having dated other celebrities. She went out with Nick Jonas from the Jonas Brothers. She also went out with Taylor Lautner. Or you might know him as Jacob from *Twilight*. Now she is dating singer Justin Bieber.

Possible Answers to the Handout: Using Complex Sentences to Link Ideas

Selena Gomez is a well-known actress. She began her career on *Barney and Friends*. Years later, she guest-starred on two shows, ~~Those shows were~~ *The Suite Life of Zack and Cody* and *Hannah Montana*. She got her big break <u>when she</u> landed the lead role <u>of Alex</u> on *Wizards of Waverly Place*. <u>But Selena is not just an actress; she is also a singer, and she has two albums out.</u> She even designed a clothing line, Dream Out Loud, <u>which</u> is sold at Kmart. Selena is also well-known for having dated other celebrities. She went out with Nick Jonas from the Jonas Brothers, <u>as well as Taylor Lautner, whom</u> you might know as Jacob from *Twilight*. Now she is dating singer Justin Bieber.

Keeping the Action Straight

Understanding Verbals

Grade Level: 8 (You can also do this lesson in grade 6 or 7, but it is not explicitly mentioned in the standards until grade 8.)

Time Frame: Approximately two class periods

Overview: This lesson shows students how to identify different types of verbals and how to avoid common usage errors with verbals. Students will apply what they learn to something they are writing for English or for another class.

Common Core State Standards

- 8: Language, Standard 1: Demonstrate command of the conventions of standard English grammar and usage when writing and speaking. a. Explain the function of verbals (gerunds, participles, infinitives) in general and their functions in particular sentences.

Objectives

- Students will learn the differences among gerunds, participles, and infinitives.

- Students will revise their essays for correct use of verbals and for parallel structure.

Background Knowledge Required

Students should have a basic understanding of the major parts of speech and how they work in sentences.

Materials Needed

- Copies of drafts that students are working on for your class or for another class. The day before you teach this lesson, remind students to bring their drafts to class.

Agenda

1. **Introduction**: Put the following sentence on the board: <u>Laughing</u> makes my face turn red. Ask students to turn to a partner and identify the part of speech of the underlined word. Share. Some students may get noun; others might say that it's a verb because "to laugh" is an action. Introducing the lesson this way allows students to make the discovery on their own. Explain that both responses are right—*laughing* is a verb form functioning as a noun. Tell students that today, you're going to discuss the different roles verbs play.

2. **Mini-Lesson**: Have students take notes on the following three types of verbals:

- Gerunds—verb forms ending in *–ing* that function as nouns.

    Example: <u>Running</u> is my favorite hobby.
    Have students suggest their own examples to add to this one.

- Infinitives—verb forms beginning with *to* that can function as nouns, adjectives, or adverbs

    Example: I love <u>to dance</u> with my new Xbox game.
    Have students suggest their own examples to add to this one.

- Participles—verb forms used as adjectives to modify nouns and pronouns

    - Present participles end in *–ing*
    - Past participles end in *–ed*
    - Participial phrases are made up of a participle and its modifiers

        Example: The balloons, <u>wrapped</u> around the tree, were starting to unravel and blow away in the wind.
        Have students suggest their own examples to add to this one.

3. **Independent Work**: Have students go through their writing to find examples of these types of verbals. They should circle and label the examples they find.

4. **Mini-Lesson**: If time remains (or the next day), talk about errors with verbals: split infinitives and errors in parallel structure.

    Split infinitives: This rule is subjective; split infinitives are not always considered wrong. However, caution students about spreading out their infinitives too much; that can make text difficult for readers to follow.

    Acceptable: Don't forget to carefully clean your lab equipment.
    Acceptable: Don't forget to clean your lab equipment carefully.
    Confusing: Don't forget to thoroughly and with great care clean your lab equipment.
    Better: Don't forget to clean your lab equipment thoroughly and with great care.

    Parallel structure: Be consistent about infinitive use.

    Not parallel and unclear: I like to swim, go running, dance, and to play soccer.
    Parallel and clearer: I like to swim, run, dance, and play soccer.

5. **Wrap-Up**: Have students go through their essays and correct such errors.

Extend the Lesson

- You can cover additional rules of parallel structure following this lesson or in separate mini-lessons. You can also have students find verbals in a text they are reading in class.

Differentiation

For students who need extra support

- Spend more time on each type of verbal before moving on to the next kind. If you have ELL students in your class, talk about what the parts of speech would be called in their language(s); this might help them understand the rules.

For advanced students

- Have them add participial phrases to their writing.

Assessment

- Evaluate students' essays for correct use of verbals.

- Check students' participation during the mini-lesson to see if they are able to come up with their own examples of different types of verbals.

Additional Resources

- Grammar at About.com offers example sentences for identifying the kinds of verbals: grammar.about.com/od/basicsentencegrammar/a/verbalswhat.htm.

- Purdue's Online Writing Lab has more on parallel structure: owl.english.purdue.edu/owl/resource/623/1/.

Notes

After implementing the lesson, reflect on what worked and what you would change the next time.

_____

_____

_____

_____

34

Should You Pass on Passive Writing?

Considering Voice

Grade Level: 8

Time Frame: Approximately one class period

Overview: This lesson teaches students the difference between active and passive voice and when one might be more appropriate than the other. You can do this lesson in grade 6 or 7, but it is not specifically mentioned in the standards until grade 8.

Common Core State Standards

- 8: Language, Standard 1: Demonstrate command of the conventions of standard English grammar and usage when writing or speaking. b. Form and use verbs in active and passive voice. d. Recognize and correct inappropriate shifts in verb voice and mood.

- 8: Language, Standard 3: Use knowledge of language and its conventions when writing, speaking, reading, or listening. a. Use verbs in active and passive voice and in the conditional and subjunctive mood to achieve particular effects (e.g., emphasizing the actor or the action; expressing uncertainty or describing a state contrary to fact).

Objectives

- Students will form and recognize active and passive voice.

- Students will examine the effects each type of voice creates.

Background Knowledge Required

Students should have knowledge of the parts of speech and how they function in a sentence.

Materials Needed

- Notebook paper

- Copies of essays that students are working on in class

Agenda

1. **Introduction**: Put these two sentences on the board.

   My dog caught the stick that I threw.
   The stick that I threw was caught by my dog.

Have students jot some notes about the differences between those two sentences. Both are grammatically correct, but does the meaning or emphasis change? How?

2. **Mini-Lesson**: Have students share their thoughts. Teach that the first one is called active voice (the subject performs the action) and the second one is called passive voice (the subject is acted upon).

    Discuss why active voice is clear and easier to read and whether there is ever an occasion to use passive voice. For example, passive voice is more common in scientific writing because it highlights the action rather than the performer (e.g., "The chemical was added to the mixture"). It is also used in news and police reports when the subject is unknown (e.g., "The car was stolen" might sound better than "Somebody stole the car").

    Warn students against switching from active to passive in the same sentence. (The Common Core State Standards talk about avoiding shifts in voice). For example, this construction is awkward: I threw a stick and a ball in the backyard. My Labrador caught the stick, and the ball was grabbed by my poodle.

3. **Independent Work**: Have students take out essays they're writing for your class or for another class. Ask them to look for sentences in passive voice. If they find any, they should either revise the sentences for active voice or justify why passive voice works better. They should also check for confusing shifts in voice.

Extend the Lesson
- Pass out copies of a local newspaper, and have students find examples of active and passive voice.

Differentiation
For students who need extra support
- Spend more time identifying the subject and predicate of a sentence.

For advanced students
- Have students practice changing parts of their essay from active to passive and vice versa. Discuss the differences.

Assessment
- Evaluate students' essays for correct use of active and passive voice.

Additional Resources
- The Purdue Online Writing Lab has additional examples of voice: owl.english.purdue.edu/owl/resource/539/01/.

Notes

After implementing the lesson, reflect on what worked and what you would change the next time.

_____

_____

_____

_____

What's Missing?

Using an Ellipsis to Indicate an Omission

Grade Level: 8

Time Frame: Approximately one class period

Overview: This lesson teaches students about a more sophisticated punctuation mark, the ellipsis. Students will learn when and why to use it. They will then apply this lesson to text-based or research-based essays they are working on in class.

Common Core State Standards

- 8: Language, Standard 2: Demonstrate command of the conventions of standard English capitalization, punctuation, and spelling when writing. a. Use punctuation (comma, ellipsis, dash) to indicate a pause or break. b. Use an ellipsis to indicate an omission.

- 8: Writing, Standard 5: With some guidance and support from peers and adults, develop and strengthen writing as needed by planning, revising, editing, rewriting, or trying a new approach.

Objectives

- Students will identify when to use ellipses.

- Students will use ellipses in their own writing.

Background Knowledge Required

Students should be familiar with basic punctuation marks (periods, question marks, quotation marks, commas, and exclamation points).

Materials Needed

- Copies of the research-based essays that students are working on (for your class or for another class). Remind them the day before to bring them in.

Agenda

1. **Independent Work:** Have students go through their essays and circle any large passages they've quoted. Students should decide whether they need complete quotations to make their points. Don't have them cut anything; ask them just to think about it.

2. **Mini-Lesson**: Go over the rules for using ellipses:

    - to omit part of the middle of a quotation (omissions of the beginning or end usually don't need ellipses)
    - to indicate a pause (usually for informal writing)
    - to indicate sarcasm or hint at something (usually for informal writing)

    Note that an ellipsis is usually formed with three dots, unless it appears at the end of a sentence; then it requires four dots—a period, no space, three dots.

3. **Wrap-Up**: Have students go back to their essays and use ellipses where necessary to reduce the lengths of their quotations. First, you may wish to show students one or two examples from a scholarly text.

Extend the Lesson

- This lesson focuses on ellipses for omissions. You can also have students experiment with ellipses in dialogue and in other creative uses to suggest sarcasm, hesitation, etc.

Differentiation

For students who need extra support

- Have students pair up with more advanced students and work on their essays together.

For advanced students

- Have them share examples of how they used ellipses with the full class so that other students can learn from their examples.

Assessment

- Evaluate students' essays for correct use of ellipses and for good judgment about how much to quote from a source.

Additional Resources

- The Grammar Girl site has a great page about the rules for using ellipses: grammar .quickanddirtytips.com/ellipsis.aspx.

Notes

After implementing the lesson, reflect on what worked and what you would change the next time.

_____

_____

_____

_____

Selecting Rich, Complex Texts for Student Reading

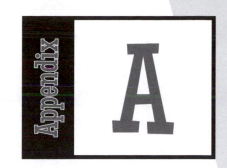

Grades 6–8

A variety of resources are available in your search for rich, complex texts for student reading. A few top-notch resources are the following:

- **American Library Association.** On the ALA website, find lists of book and media award winners that are on-level for middle school readers. Go to the Book, Print, and Media Awards page, and in the menu at the left, select the subcategory Children and Young Adults. Examples are the Alex Awards, the Booklist Editor's Choice: Books for Youth, Booklist Editor's Choice: Media, Coretta Scott King Book Award, Notable Children's Recordings, Great Web Sites for Kids, and Newbery Medal winners. Go to www.ala.org/awardsgrants/awards/browse/bpma?showfilter=no.

- **Appendix B of the Common Core State Standards for English Language Arts & Literacy in History/Social Studies, Science, and Technical Subjects.** The appendix lists nearly 50 exemplar texts grouped by genre and includes excerpts of each. You'll notice an emphasis on classic literature by Louisa May Alcott, Mark Twain, Walt Whitman, Langston Hughes, and others, as well as informational texts on topics in social studies, science, math, and technology. Go to www.corestandards.org/assets/Appendix_B.pdf. *Note: These lists are merely suggestions and are in no way mandatory. Teachers should feel confident in choosing sources other than these exemplar texts.*

- **Association for Library Service to Children.** The ALSC maintains lists of notable books and media for children. Go to www.ala.org/alsc/awardsgrants.

- *Children and Libraries* is the journal of the Association for Library Services to Children. Browse it for recommendation-packed articles on poetry, biography, historical fiction, culturally diverse fiction and nonfiction, and more.

- **EBSCO***host.* Check to see if your school or public library subscribes to this searchable database. It includes full-text articles from magazines and newspapers as well as e-books and audio books. To learn more about resources for middle school readers, go to http://ebscohost.com/us-middle-schools.

- **The Horn Book.** *The Horn Book Magazine* has short reviews (some starred) of current fiction, poetry and song, nonfiction, and audio books, with each review noting one or two reading levels: primary, intermediate, middle school, or high school. *The Horn Book Guide* is a semi-annual publication (print and online) that rates and reviews titles published in the previous six months, indexed for ease of use. Go to www.hbook.com.

- **The Junior Library Guild** creates lists of outstanding books, national- and state-award winners, and themes (e.g., summer reading, women's history) for middle school and junior high. Browsing the Guild's backlist of titles is also useful, and you can sort the list by reading level and genre by using the Advanced Search feature. Go to www.juniorlibraryguild.com, click on Books & Levels, then click on Backlist Catalog. While the lists are aimed at librarians who want to expand their collections, they are equally useful to teachers.

- **Lexile Framework for Reading.** To get lists of books that are leveled at grade level (or just below or just above), you can go to www.lexile.com, type in the grade you teach, choose book topics, and click Submit. You can sort for a wide range of topics, including biography, social issues, science and technology, graphic novels, animals, nature, fairy tales, and more. You can also type in the title of a book in the Quick Book Search box to find out its Lexile measure. For example, the measure for *Vincent Van Gogh: Portrait of an Artist* by Jan Greenberg and Sandra Jordan is 1100L, which corresponds to the upper range of the grade 8 reading level. This book, then, would be suitable for advanced readers early in the eighth-grade year and would be an ideal complex text for all readers at the end of that year.

- **Librarians.** Children's and youth librarians are usually enthusiastic about compiling lists of quality texts for teachers, given sufficient lead time. You might request nonfiction texts at a specific reading level, for example, or an assortment of fiction and nonfiction on a topic such as the Industrial Revolution, child workers, or sweatshops. You might need books or articles with maps, charts, diagrams, and timelines. Even if you don't need an entire reading list, librarians (who spend hours reading reviews of books in catalogs and journals) are happy to help you identify reputable texts that will serve a specific teaching purpose.

- **Library of Congress.** The LOC has online collections of historic newspapers, prints and photographs, sounds recordings, maps, manuscripts, and primary source documents, all of which can help you meet requirements of the Common Core State Standards. Go to www.loc.gov/index.html to browse collections. Also, on that page, look for the "Especially for" menu, and click on Teachers. Here you'll find primary source sets for classroom use and a link to the *Teaching with Primary Sources Journal*, available online.

- *Middle and Junior High Core Collection.* Ask a local librarian if you can peruse the library's copy of H. W. Wilson Publishing Company's *Middle and Junior High Core Collection*. This resource annotates and evaluates fiction, nonfiction, story collections, and magazines for grades 5 to 9. According to the company's website, "Among nonfiction entries, special importance is given to works devoted to technology, personal values, and current social and political issues, with special emphasis on ethnic diversity. Fiction entries encompass a broad spectrum of classics as well as contemporary fiction and genre literature [and] literary works that are of interest to young readers, including many titles that are frequently part of the school curriculum." *Note: The word* Core *in the title does not refer to the Common Core.*

- **Scholastic News Magazines.** Scholastic publishes classroom magazines leveled to student readers and correlated to Common Core standards. The texts increase in difficulty as the year progresses. *Scholastic Scope, Scholastic Action, Choices,* and *The New York Times Upfront* are a few examples. Depending on the magazine, the texts are informational or a variety of text types and may include charts, graphs, maps, and links to online videos. Go to http://classroommagazines.scholastic.com to see all the magazines; look for the link to Common Core information.

- *School Library Journal.* Ask a school librarian if you can peruse a few copies of this monthly journal. The year-end Best Books issue is helpful. In any issue, flip to "The Book Review." Look for starred reviews in the subsections for Grades 5 & Up (fiction and nonfiction) and for Graphic Novels. For example, in the January 2008 issue, a starred review of J. Patrick Lewis's *The Brothers' War: Civil War Voices in Verse* is recommended for grades 7 and up and includes a map, photos, reproductions, and a chronology. Informational paragraphs accompany reproduced images of the war. Special review sections in the journal focus on topics such as black history. In the January 2008 issue, Barbara Wysocki's "Cold Comfort" reviews websites, DVDs, fiction, and nonfiction on the topic of the Arctic for readers up through grade 8 (pages 55–59).

- **Smithsonian Institution.** The Smithsonian has online resources for educators, including curricula, print materials, multimedia, and videos for loan. Topics include American history, inventions and innovation, American art, African art, air and space, and more. Find the home page for educators at www.si.edu/Educators. In addition, the page for researchers has links to resources such as the *Encyclopedia Smithsonian*, an online encyclopedia suitable for student use. The Online Collections and Databases may also be of use. The research home page is at www.si.edu/Researchers.

- **State and regional library associations** sponsor book awards. For example, in California, four statewide organizations committed to literacy sponsor the California Young Reader Medal. The yearly list of nominees totals nearly 20 titles covering five categories, including Middle School/Junior High and Picture Books for Older Readers. Another example is the Young Readers Choice Awards administered by the Pacific Northwest Library Association. See details at www.pnla.org/yrca. A librarian at your school or local library can give you information on your state's or region's award program and help you find the book lists from other programs.

Sample Argument Writing Prompts

Grades 6–8

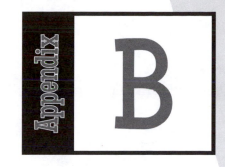

While acknowledging the importance of informative and narrative writing, the Common Core introduces a special emphasis on argument writing in grades 6–8. The following writing prompts, organized by grade level, are intended to provide ideas and inspiration as you incorporate argument writing into your curriculum.

Feel free to modify these samples to fit your teaching purposes. You can adapt most prompts to a different grade by adding or removing specific criteria in a grade's writing standard. Each grade's argument-writing standard is included in full, for easy reference.

To create your own prompts, keep this tip in mind: Build the writing task around an arguable claim. Some claims are controversial, while others are simply open to multiple interpretations or points of view. The essential quality is that it be a statement or idea that people can disagree about. Students should support the claim with evidence rather than simply appealing to the emotions of the reader. In grades 7 and 8, students should also address counterclaims.

You can create short writing tasks by having students write for five minutes in response to a pro-or-con, either-or, or yes-or-no prompt. An example is "Should all public schools be required to create a green space, such as a garden, to help protect the environment?" Responses could be T-charts or freewriting. These quick tasks let students focus on articulating an arguable claim and identifying a supporting reason or two. In contrast, the longer writing tasks that follow require students to produce more sophisticated written responses.

Grade 6 students:

Write arguments to support claims with clear reasons and relevant evidence.

a. Introduce claim(s) and organize the reasons and evidence clearly.

b. Support claim(s) with clear reasons and relevant evidence, using credible sources and demonstrating an understanding of the topic or text.

c. Use words, phrases, and clauses to clarify the relationship among claim(s) and reasons.

d. Establish and maintain a formal style.

e. Provide a concluding statement or section that follows from the argument presented.

(Writing Standard 1)

Grade 6

While these prompts are written with student readers in mind, they may contain vocabulary (such as *connotation, enhance,* and *hinder*) that needs clarifying before students begin to write.

Writing Prompt 1

Context for Writing: This prompt works well in conjunction with reading a poem or narrative that has multiple examples of figurative and connotative language. Before assigning the prompt, review figurative language and the concept of word connotations.

Writing Task: Think about the story (poem) that you read. Does the author's use of figurative language and connotations enhance or hinder the reader's understanding of the text? Write a paper to explain your opinion.

- Introduce the topic of figurative language and connotations. Give the title and author of the work.

- State your opinion about the author's use of figurative language and connotations.

- Give **three** clear reasons to make your opinion convincing. *Tip:* Use words such as *consequently* and *therefore* to link reasons to your opinion.

- Support each reason with details or examples from the text. Use at least **one** direct quotation from the text to support a reason.

- Give your paper a concluding sentence or paragraph. *Tip:* Use a phrase such as *for these reasons* or *as these reasons show* to introduce a restatement of your opinion.

- Don't forget to give your paper an interesting title!

Writing Prompt 2

Context for Writing: Use this prompt in conjunction with a discussion of a moral lesson or statement about society in a work of fiction or a biography. Make sure that students identify a lesson or statement as opposed to just a topic. For instance, a moral lesson is "A tragedy can destroy you, or it can make you leave your cocoon to become to butterfly," while a topic is "facing tragedy."

Writing Task: Write an argument about a moral lesson or statement about society in the story you read. Do you claim that the moral or statement is realistic or unrealistic?

- In the introduction, give the story's title and author and a brief summary of the plot. Identify the moral lesson or statement about society. State your claim: Is the moral or statement about society realistic or unrealistic? *Tip:* Give information in an order that makes sense; for instance, you might want to identify the moral before summarizing the plot.

- In the body of the argument, give reasons to support your claim. Support and explain each reason with details from the story. Use at least **one** direct quotation from the story. *Tip:* Link ideas by using connectors such as *because, for instance,* or *for example.*

- Bring the argument to a close by restating your claim or telling why your claim should matter to other readers.

- Be sure to give your paper an interesting title!

Writing Prompt 3

Context for Writing: Use this prompt after students compare and contrast two versions of the same event. (The event could be an event of national importance or an event in the life of a person such as Anne Frank or Nikki Giovanni.)

Writing Task: Both texts tell about the same event. Which text does a better job helping the reader understand the event? Write an argument to prove your point of view.

- Introduce the event. In a few sentences, sum up what happened.

- Give the titles and authors of the two texts you read.

- State your claim. Which text does a better job of telling what happened?

- Give reasons to support your opinion. Use examples and details from the text to make your reasons clear. *Tip:* Use words and phrases such as *for instance* and *for example* to link reasons to supporting details.

- Arrange information clearly. For example, give one reason, along with supporting details, in each paragraph.

- Give a concluding statement or paragraph. For example, tell why people who are interested in this topic would want to read this text.

- Revise your work to make sure you avoid slang, contractions, and other examples of informal writing.

- Give your paper a title that makes your topic or your claim clear.

Writing Prompt 4

Context for Writing: Show *The Miracle Worker* (a biography of Helen Keller) in class, following it with a discussion of the role of sign language in the improvement of Helen's life. Provide (or have students gather) statistics about the use of sign language in the United States. If your school has policies about language classes and clubs, share those.

Writing Task: Do you think sign language should be offered as a class in school or as a school club? Why or why not? Write an argument to prove your point of view on this topic.

- Introduce the topic of sign language and state your claim: Should sign language be offered as a class or club in school?

- Give reasons to support your claim. Support each reason with details from the film and from the statistics and class discussion about sign language. *Tip:* Link ideas by using connectors such as *because, for instance,* or *for example.*

- Bring the argument to a close by making a final statement that reinforces your claim.

- Revise your work to make sure you avoid slang, contractions, and other examples of informal writing.

- Give your paper a title that makes your topic or your claim clear.

Writing Prompt 5

Context for Writing: Use this prompt in conjunction with a full-class discussion on the theme "room for improvement in our school." You might suggest topics such as nutrition, respect, fun, safety, cleanliness, or school spirit.

Writing Task: From your point of view, what part of your school most needs improvement? Write a letter to your principal to convince him or her to make one important improvement in your school.

- Introduce your topic and explain what most needs improvement in your school.

- Give strong reasons to support your point of view. Support each reason with facts, details, and examples about your school.

- Use connectors to link ideas. Some examples are *first, next, more important, because of this problem,* and *specifically.* You can come up with other connectors, too.

- Give your letter a strong conclusion. What is the main idea you want your principal to remember?

- Use the format of a formal letter, which begins with "Dear" and your principal's name, and concludes with "Sincerely" and your name. Avoid slang, contractions, silly jokes, and other examples of informal writing.

Grade 7 students:

Write arguments to support claims with clear reasons and relevant evidence.

a. Introduce claim(s), acknowledge alternate or opposing claims, and organize the reasons and evidence logically.

b. Support claim(s) with logical reasoning and relevant evidence, using accurate, credible sources and demonstrating an understanding of the topic or text.

c. Use words, phrases, and clauses to create cohesion and clarify the relationship among claim(s), reasons, and evidence.

d. Establish and maintain a formal style.

e. Provide a concluding statement or section that follows from and supports the argument presented.

Grade 7

As with the Grade 6 prompts, these are written with student readers in mind, although they may contain vocabulary that needs clarifying before students begin to write.

Writing Prompt 1

Context for Writing: Read one or more accounts that show a person or people using violence to combat an oppressor. An example is the scene in *Narrative of the Life of Frederick Douglass* in which Douglass fights back physically against the slave owner. Another example is the Boston Tea Party (destruction of property). You might choose to use contemporary news articles.

Writing Task: Is violence ever an acceptable response to mistreatment? Write an argument to express your point of view.

▪ Introduce the topic of violence as a response to mistreatment. You might want to summarize a scene from a text you read to show your readers exactly what you mean.

▪ State your claim, or point of view, about using violence.

▪ Support your claim with clear reasons.

▪ Explain each reason with facts, examples, or details from the text. Include at least **two** direct quotations from the text. *Tip:* Use conjunctions such as *therefore, consequently, as a result,* and *for this reason* to show how ideas relate.

▪ Revise your work to make sure you avoid slang, contractions, and other examples of informal writing.

▪ Give your paper a title that makes your topic or claim clear.

Writing Prompt 2

Context for Writing: Use this prompt in conjunction with a full-class discussion on the topic of technology in classrooms. What kinds of technology do classrooms in your school need? What are the top three priorities? Why are they higher priorities than others?

Writing Task: From your point of view, what type of technology most needs to be added to classrooms in your school? Write a letter to your principal to convince him or her to make this improvement in your school.

- Introduce your topic and identify what technology should be added to classrooms in your school.

- Give strong reasons to support your point of view. Support each reason with facts, details, and examples about your school and about the technology you chose.

- Address at least one opposing viewpoint, showing why it is weak or erroneous.

- Use phrases to organize and link ideas. Some examples are *one reason, another reason,* and *the most important reason.*

- Give your letter a strong conclusion. What is the main idea you want your principal to remember?

- Use the format of a formal letter, which begins with "Dear" and your principal's name, and concludes with "Sincerely" and your name. Avoid slang, contractions, insults, and other examples of informal writing.

Writing Prompt 3

Context for Writing: Have students read a book and watch a film about the book. Have them do prewriting or discussions in which they compare the effects of techniques in each medium. Techniques might include dialogue, narrative voice, description, sound, camera angle, or others.

Writing Task: Write an argument in which you prove which version of the story is more effective, the book or the film.

- Introduce the book, giving its title and author, and the film, giving its title and director. State your claim about which version of the story is better.

- Support your claim with clear reasons. Explain each reason with facts, examples, or details from the book or film. *Tip:* Use conjunctions such as *because, in contrast, consequently,* and *furthermore* to show how ideas relate.

- Mention at least one viewpoint that opposes your claim or one of your reasons. Explain why your point of view makes more sense.

- Revise your work to make sure you avoid slang, contractions, and other examples of informal writing.

- Give your paper a title that makes your topic or claim clear.

Writing Prompt 4

Context for Writing: Have students read an opinion text such as an op-ed piece, a letter to the editor, or a blog. In a class discussion, determine the author's point of view on the topic and analyze how the author explains or defends the point of view.

Writing Task: Think about the opinion text that you read. Do you agree or disagree with the author's point of view? Write an argument to express your point of view.

- Include an introduction that summarizes the topic and gives the title and author of the text you read. State your claim, or point of view, on the topic.

- Give reasons to make your claim clear and convincing. Expand on each reason by giving details, facts, quotes, or examples from the text. If you wish, find another text on the same topic that will help you defend your point of view, and use information from it, too. Include at least **one** direct quotation from one of the texts.

- Any debatable topic supports more than one point of view. What is a strong reason to *oppose* your point of view? What do you have to say in response? Include a few sentences or a paragraph to deal with an opposing viewpoint.

- Revise your argument to show careful use of language. For one thing, make sure to use formal English and correct grammar. Also, use words and phrases such as *however, unfortunately, in addition, most important,* etc., to show how your ideas relate.

- Conclude your argument with a strong final thought that links to your claim.

- Make sure to give your paper a title that connects to the topic or your claim.

Writing Prompt 5

Context for Writing: Have students read about or research banned books in middle schools.

Writing Task: Is it acceptable for schools to ban certain books in it classrooms? Or should teachers have full freedom to choose the books they teach? Write an argument to express your point of view on this topic.

- Include an introduction that explains the topic of banned books and presents the two sides of the argument. State your claim, or point of view, on the topic.

- Give reasons to make your claim clear and convincing. Expand on each reason by giving details, facts, quotes, or examples from one or more texts.

- Any debatable topic supports more than one point of view. What is a strong reason to *oppose* your point of view? What do you have to say in response? Include a few sentences or a paragraph to deal with an opposing viewpoint.

- Revise your argument to show careful organization of ideas. You might organize the paragraphs as a series of sample scenarios, each one about a different book. Another idea is to list and explain reasons that apply to books in general, and mention a few books as examples. A third idea is to use a problem-and-solution structure: First, identify the problem (banning books or allowing too much freedom); then, argue for a smart way to solve this problem.

- Conclude your argument with a strong final thought that links to your claim.

- Make sure to give your paper a title that connects to the topic or your claim.

Grade 8 students:

Write arguments to support claims with clear reasons and relevant evidence.

a. Introduce claim(s), acknowledge and distinguish the claim(s) from alternate or opposing claims, and organize the reasons and evidence logically.

b. Support claim(s) with logical reasoning and relevant evidence, using accurate, credible sources and demonstrating an understanding of the topic or text.

c. Use words, phrases, and clauses to create cohesion and clarify the relationship among claim(s), counterclaims, reasons, and evidence.

d. Establish and maintain a formal style.

e. Provide a concluding statement or section that follows from and supports the argument presented.

(Writing Standard 1)

Grade 8

As with the prompts for previous grades, these are written with student readers in mind, although they may contain vocabulary that needs clarifying before students begin to write.

Writing Prompt 1

Context for Writing: Have a full-class discussion about how students spend their free time on a typical Saturday afternoon. Should every minute be scheduled for maximum fun? Should the television stay turned off? Should the time be devoted to family—or friends? What is the best use of a Saturday afternoon? Then, have students research to answer a question such as "How much time does the average teenager spend watching television?" or "What percentage of teenagers play sports in their spare time?" or "What percentage of teenagers read in their spare time?" Students may want to team up with someone writing on the same topic and perform the research task together.

Writing Task: Write a letter to your class as a whole. Use the letter to prove your point of view on the best way to spend a Saturday afternoon.

- Introduce your topic and state your claim about the best way to spend a Saturday afternoon.

- Give strong reasons to support your point of view. Support each reason with facts, details, and examples about young people your age. Use at least **two** direct quotations from a text you researched.

- Address at least one opposing viewpoint, defending your claim against it.

- Use phrases to organize and link ideas. Some examples are *one reason, another reason,* and *the most important reason.*

- Give your letter a strong conclusion. What is the main idea you want your classmates to remember?

- Use the format of a formal letter, and avoid slang, contractions, insults, and other examples of informal writing.

Writing Prompt 2

Context for Writing: Before assigning this prompt, have students read 2–3 short news or magazine articles about the use of cell phones in public. Conduct a full-class discussion about talking and texting on phones in public. What, if any, should the limitations be? Consider locations such as streets and highways, schools, libraries, movie theaters, church services, doctors' offices, and so on.

Writing Task: What limits, if any, should be placed on the use of cell phones in public? Write an argument to prove your point of view.

- Introduce the topic of cell phone use in public. You might want to hook your reader's interest with a short scenario about someone using a cell phone in public.

- State your claim, or point of view, about cell phone use in public.

- Write several paragraphs that support your claim with clear reasons. Explain each reason with facts, examples, or details from the articles you read. Include at least **one** direct quotation from an article. *Tip:* Organize your reasons so that they lead up to the strongest or most important. For instance, if you think using a cell phone while crossing a street could be deadly, give this reason last.

- Revise your work to make sure you avoid slang, contractions, and other examples of informal writing.

- Give your paper a title that makes your topic or your claim clear.

Writing Prompt 3

Context for Writing: Have students examine two or more mediums that present the same topic or idea. Examples are a print text, a digital text, a video, a podcast, an audio book, and a film.

Writing Task: Consider the different mediums that you examined. Which one does the best job of presenting the topic or idea? Write an argument to prove your point of view.

- In your introduction, give details about the mediums you compared and the topic or idea they share. State your claim about which medium does the best job of presenting the topic or idea.

- Give reasons to make your claim clear and convincing. Expand on each reason by giving details, facts, quotes, or examples from one or both of the mediums. *Tip:* Use connecting words and phrases such as *for example, another reason, in addition,* and *however* to link ideas in sentences or to provide a transition between paragraphs.

- Any debatable topic supports more than one point of view. What is a strong reason to *oppose* your point of view? What do you have to say in response? Include a few sentences or a paragraph to deal with an opposing viewpoint.

- Revise your argument to a formal writing style throughout the paper.

- Conclude your argument with a strong final thought that links to your claim.

- Make sure to give your paper a title that connects to the topic or your claim.

Writing Prompt 4

Context for Writing: Use this writing prompt in conjunction with reading a narrative that features at least two well-developed characters (a story, novel, drama, or poem will work well).

Writing Task: Consider the characters in the work of literature that you read. In your opinion, which character is most convincing as a "real" person? Write an argument to prove your point of view.

- Introduce the title of the work, the author, and the characters you compared. State your claim about which character is most convincing as a "real" person.

- Give reasons to make your claim clear and convincing. For example, what do you mean by "real person," and how does the character fulfill your expectations?

- Use details, facts, quotes, or examples from the text to support and explain the reasons why you chose this character. Remember that each reason you give must be supported by evidence from the text.

- What might someone say in opposition to your point of view? How can you defend your point of view against the opposing claim(s)? Include a few sentences or a paragraph to deal with one or more opposing viewpoints.

- Revise your argument to a formal writing style throughout the paper. For example, make sure to write in complete sentences, use paragraph breaks, and use standard English grammar.

- Conclude your argument with a strong final thought that links to your claim.

- Make sure to give your paper a title that connects to the topic or your claim.

Writing Prompt 5

Context for Writing: Have students read a persuasive historical speech or letter. In a class discussion, determine the author's point of view and analyze how the author supports the point of view.

Writing Task: Think about the text that you read. Is the author's point of view convincing? Why or why not? Write an argument to prove your judgment of the text's effectiveness.

- Include an introduction that gives the title and author of the text and identifies the author's main idea. State your claim, or judgment, about whether the text effectively persuades readers to accept the author's point of view.

- Give reasons to make your claim clear and convincing. Expand on each reason by giving details, facts, quotes, or examples from the text. Include at least **two** direct quotations from the text.

- Any debatable topic supports more than one point of view. What is a strong reason to *oppose* your claim? What do you have to say in response to the opposition? Include a few sentences or a paragraph to deal with an opposing viewpoint.

- Revise your argument to show careful use of language. For one thing, make sure to use formal English and correct grammar. Also, use words and phrases such as *however, unfortunately, in addition, most important,* etc., to show how your ideas relate.

- Conclude your argument with a strong final thought that links to your claim.

- Make sure to give your paper a title that connects to the topic or your claim.

Blank Lesson Plan Template

Use the following template to create your own Common Core lesson plans in reading, writing, speaking/listening, and language. Remember that your lessons should be integrated when possible and cover more than one standard.

Topic/Title: _____

Grade Level:

Time Frame:

Overview:

Common Core State Standards

-
-
-
-

Objectives

-
-
-
-

Background Knowledge Required

Materials Needed

-
-
-
-

Agenda

1.

2.

3.

4.

5.

Extend the Lesson

-
-

Differentiation

For students who need extra support

-
-

For advanced students

-
-

Assessment

-
-
-
-

Additional Resources

-
-

Notes

After implementing the lesson, reflect on what worked and what you would change the next time.

_____

_____

_____

_____

References

Arechiga, Debbie (2012). *Reaching English language learners in every classroom: Energizers for teaching and learning*. Larchmont, NY: Eye On Education.

Benjamin, A., & Crow, J. T. (2013). *Vocabulary at the core: Teaching the Common Core Standards*. Larchmont, NY: Eye On Education.

Blackburn, B. R. (2012). *Rigor made easy: Getting started*. Larchmont, NY: Eye On Education.

Calkins, L., Ehrenworth, M., & Lehman, C. (2012). *Pathways to the Common Core: Accelerating achievement*. Portsmouth, NH: Heinemann.

Coleman, D. & Pimentel, S. (2012). *Revised publishers' criteria for the Common Core State Standards in English language arts and literacy, grades 3–12*. Washington, D.C.: The National Association of State Boards of Education, Council of Chief State School Officers, Achieve, and the Council of the Great City Schools.

Hemingway, Ernest (1953). "A Day's Wait." In *The short stories of Ernest Hemingway* (pp. 436–437). New York: Charles Scribner's Sons.

National Governors Association Center for Best Practices, Council of Chief State School Officers (2010). *Common Core State Standards for English language arts*. Washington, D.C.: National Governors Association Center for Best Practices, Council of Chief State School Officers. Retrieved from www.corestandards.org/the-standards.

Roberts, T., & Billings, L. (2012). *Teaching critical thinking: Using seminars for 21st century literacy*. Larchmont, NY: Eye On Education.

Silverstein, Shel (1964). *The giving tree*. New York: Harper and Row.

Walker, Alice (1988). "Really, *Doesn't* Crime Pay?" In A. Landy (Ed.), *The Heath introduction to literature, 3rd ed.* (p. 180). Lexington, MA: D. C. Heath and Company.

Wolpert-Gawron, H. (2011). *'Tween crayons and curfews: Tips for middle school teachers*. Larchmont, NY: Eye On Education.

Notes

Notes

Notes

Notes

Notes

Notes

Notes